A MAVERICK'S GUIDE TO THE LAW OF ATTRACTION, BOOK 1

Energy Creates

Lisa Rasche

Amazon KDP Publishing

CONTENTS

MEDICAL AND LEGAL DISCLAIMER

This work is solely for personal growth and education. It should not be treated as a substitute for professional assistance or medical advice. It is sold with the understanding that the author and publisher are not engaged in rendering medical, psychological, financial, legal, or other professional services. The reader should consult his/her medical, health, or other competent professional before adopting any of the suggestions in this book or deriving inferences from it. The application of protocols or information in this book is the choice of each reader, who assumes full responsibility for his or her understandings, interpretations, and results. The author and publisher assume no responsibility for the actions or choices of any reader.

INTRODUCTION: THE JOURNEY FROM WANTING TO GETTING

This book is not for beginners.

If you've never heard of the Law of Attraction, you're better off finding a beginner's guide.

This book is for those who have had some success with the Law of Attraction (LOA)...but also a lot of failures. It's for those who have some stuck places that don't seem to budge no matter how many visualizations or affirmations they do.

The reason we hit a wall with regular LOA books is because most of them don't address what really creates: energy.

It's not your pretty mental pictures that create. It's not your happy shiny feelings that create. It's not your peppy positive thoughts that create.

Energy creates.

This book will dive deep into energy work, helping you shift the stuck places of your life from crummy, frustrating 3D energy to high-flying 5D energy. We'll cover what 3D, 4D, and 5D energy are, how to shift from one to another, and how to tune in energetically to what you want to manifest.

A lot of the material will question what other LOA teachers say. Just because something is traditional in the Law of Attraction world doesn't mean it's right for you. You have to be willing to question and try things out for yourself. That's why I call it a "maverick's guide." The heart of being a LOA maverick is: Take what resonates with you, and leave the rest. (That goes for everything in this book, by the way!)

Before we dive deep, what is the basic structure of a manifestation?

As Source energy--as souls, or spirits, or floppy-winged angels, or whatever sort of being you think we are on the Other Side of the veil--we instantly get what we want. You think of it, and it's there. No delay. No patience required. Instant manifestation. After all, you are connected with all things, and on the Other Side, you know it. You know that backwards and forwards, and it's no trouble to get what you want the moment you want it, the same way you would in a lucid dream. Fun, right?

For a while, at least. But after zapping two-story ice cream sundaes into existence a million times, and having every water-skiing shark-jumping adventure you want, you want something new. Souls start wanting what they can't really have on the Other Side: surprises, suspense, drama. Just imagine what Cinderella's story would be as a super-manifesting hotshot on the Other Side:

Cinderella wanted a fierce dress and a prince. Instantly, she got them. The End.

Not much of a story, is it? Fun for a while, but pretty soon we get curious about having a little more edge to the tale, a slower crescendo to happiness, a wilder ride. In order to have a real Cinderella story (and most other stories we are interested in), we've got to create space between *wanting* something and *getting* it.

That journey from wanting to getting is the exciting part you can't experience while you're a super-powerful instantaneous manifesting soul-creature on the Other Side. But how *do* you create that gap between wanting and getting, when every energy of the universe bends instantly to your call and promotes your desire with full force at every moment?

You need a realm where energy is denser and slower. When energy is slow and dense, your intentions do not instantly manifest, and you can create a gap between deciding you want something and actually experiencing it.

Those slow, often resistant energies help you make a fun story, a story where Cinderella has to hang out in the garden with mice, waiting with a wish and a prayer, swabbing floors and trying to be polite to crusty stepsisters, slow-dancing under a chandelier with a handsome prince and wondering how it's all going to turn out at midnight.

While most of the universe's higher energies are hauling butt trying to bring Cinderella's prince to her, the wise Cinderella-Soul has enlisted other, denser energies to slow that delivery down. Rude family, dirty housework, low self-esteem, doubts about whether dreams come true? All these things are helping create the story. They're holding the arrival of her prince back so that there *is* a story. They are keeping it from being another humdrum instant manifestation. They are giving her a journey from wanting to getting.

Most of the times you want something--especially if it's something meaningful to your heart--some part of you is also drumming up some energies to push against your dream, so that you don't get it too quickly or unsatisfyingly. These energies are what we call resistance, and they are prevalent on Planet Earth. They can take the form of outer obstacles, like a snippy stepmom who demands excessive chores. Or they can take the form of inner obstacles, like fears that no one will ever love you or beliefs that fairy godmothers don't exist.

Resistance is energy that is actually trying to help you. We think of it as something to hurry and get rid of, but it's doing what it's doing *for* us, just like all energy in the universe. It's playing the role of the devil's advocate or the mustache-twirling villain, so that you have an interesting ride to your success instead of another ho-hum instant manifestation.

Planet Earth is sooooo good at drumming up this "helpfully unhelpful" slow, resistant energy. Here, it's all over the place, and it's ready to help spin out the story of you getting your desire with lots of roller coaster ups and downs, plot twists, and bizarre midnight deadlines.

The reason why so many souls come to this planet to have their "slowly getting my desire" experience is because this planet is set up to provide you lots and lots of slow, dense energy to delay your manifestations. In fact, there are so many resistant energies here that you might not ever get what you want. Now that's mystery! Will Cinderella get her prince? On the Other Side, it's definite. On Planet Earth, it's a maybe, and a show worth watching.

Not only will Cinderella-Soul be able to enter Earth programmed with a lot of resistance (low self-esteem thanks to her culture, beliefs that magic doesn't happen thanks to the collective unconscious, distractions of pain, hunger, and itching thanks to her biological body), but also she'll have to contend with the free will choices of other players doing their own stories. The prince, her family, and every random villager may decide to do something Cinderella-Soul didn't expect. There is resistance all over the place.

Of course, now that folks like you and I are immersed in this planetary environment, we're not clasping our hands and saying, "Oh no, what if I get my desire too easily? How dull that would be!" That was what our souls were originally concerned about, but Planet Earth is so good at what it does, we no longer have *that* worry. The source of our stress isn't that our desires arrive "too dang fast"--quite the opposite!

Our souls wanted some drama, some obstacles, some delays. Check, check, check. We've got all that--and more than we really wanted, usually. But it's helpful to acknowledge that the things holding us back from our dreams are just energy. And this energy isn't some malevolent thing trying to make us miserable, and it's not us "messing up," either. It's energy that *wants* to help us, but it's helping by being a slow medium for our intentions to pass through.

So long as you're on this planet, you're unlikely to get

everything you want instantly. There's an atmosphere of energy designed to hold us back some, though that is lessening day by day. A little bit of a slowdown helps us enjoy action.

How fun is it doing a crossword puzzle when you know every answer instantly? (Here's a hint: you probably already can do this with elementary school crosswords. What's a three-letter word for "an animal that goes 'meow'"?) You're not spending your free time doing little-kid puzzles because it's just not fun when you can instantly fill in every blank.

Most of the fun of eating your favorite dish is that it takes time and the action of chewing, swallowing, and so on. You wouldn't really want it to be eaten instantaneously. The action is part of the fun. So on this planet, we can expect that in general, our creations won't be instantaneous, and in general, they will involve some kind of enjoyable action.

So now we've covered the basic journey from wanting to getting:

You want something. Your intention goes out for it.

Planet Earth's dense energy slows that intention down, creating obstacles and delays of various kinds.

Other people add their intentions to the mix, creating further obstacles and delays (or speeding it up, if they're helpful folks).

At this point, you can take your chances and let things play out as they will. Maybe your manifestation will happen, maybe it won't, depending on all the resistant energy involved.

But if you'd like a better method, I suggest the one I'll describe in this book:

Shift your energy around the topic from the obstacle-ridden 3D energy you've probably got...

...to the high-flying 5D energy that manifests intentions much quicker.

To do this, you need to know what 3D, 4D, and 5D energy are. That's Section 1.

You'll also need to know how to sense what kind of energy you have. That's Section 2.

You'll also need some tools for actually making the shift to 5D. That's Section 3.

If you want extra tools for manifesting something specific, Section 4 will provide those. But they won't make a lot of sense without the background in the previous sections.

I hope this perspective on the Law of Attraction will help you understand why manifestations often seem hit or miss.

As always, take what resonates and leave the rest.

SECTION 1: THE QUALITY OF ENERGY YOU HAVE AROUND A TOPIC

DIMENSIONS OF ENERGETIC CONSCIOUSNESS: 3D, 4D, AND 5D

We want to be able to manifest our desires faster, despite the slow, dense energy of Earth. How do we do that?

It turns out, different layers of consciousness can help or hinder your desired manifestation. The slow energy that gives us a gap between wanting and getting is 3D energy. Planet Earth has existed in the 3D realm for a long time. 3D means the third density, or the third dimension, depending on whom you ask. "Dimension" here doesn't really mean the kind of dimensions mathematicians or physicists talk about. It's just a metaphor for consciousness, not literal dimensions.

Similarly, take the numbering system (3D, 4D, etc.) with a grain of salt. In reality, consciousness is a continuum. Depending on how you divide up the continuum, you may say there are three levels, or seven levels, or twenty, or one hundred...it just depends on how thinly you slice your levels. So if you read about "4D" being somewhat different than how I describe it in some other person's book, it doesn't necessarily mean that one of us is wrong. It may be that we are slicing up the continuum a little differently. I'm going to call these slices of dimensions 3D, 4D, and 5D, but in another person's system they could be labelled 3.1, 3.2, and 3.3, or 140, 150, and 160...it really doesn't matter how you slice it. It's more important to notice the progression consciousness goes through as it rises than to fuss about which label is used.

That said, here's how I divide up the consciousness continuum for the purposes of this book. Earth has a lot of dense, slow, heavy energy, filled with a lot of negativity. That's 3D.

4D is somewhat faster, lighter energy. It still creates a gap between wanting and getting, but not so big a gap as 3D. It's a happier vibration for the likes of souls like us. There is more of this energy on Earth now than there has been in the past.

5D is very high, very fast energy, but still vibrating slowly enough for there to be physical bodies. 5D consciousness is usually experienced as blissful love for souls that get there. There is very little negativity in 5D. Although it still slows down your intentions slightly, the gap between wanting and getting becomes very small in 5D. 5D is still rare on Earth, but it's getting more and more traction than before.

There are other densities, both lower and higher, but these three--3D, 4D, and 5D--are the ones relevant for human beings and most other life on Earth. Each density has a way of life that is natural to it. Each density makes certain experiences very likely and others less likely. In general, human history has started out in 3D and is currently moving up into 4D and 5D.

3D is the slow, heavy space that has made a lot of our adventures possible. Souls that were curious about negativity came to explore 3D. Although human beings are moving from 3D to 4D to 5D, in reality, there is no hierarchy. All the levels are valuable and interesting in their own way.

We talk about moving "up" to 4D, or 5D being a "higher" vibration, but that's really just to say that most humans prefer 4D and 5D right now. In the past, high-vibrational souls like yours got very interested in moving "down" to 3D, where you could finally explore that fascinating thing called negativity you'd heard so much about! It was a way to narrow in on certain effects of creation. 3D was the goal back then. But now, most human beings want a lighter, happier, more loving life, and that means we are angled towards 5D. 5D isn't better in some cosmic sense. It's just where we happen to want to go now.

In other words, the labels of "upper" and "lower" are not meant as judgy labels of goodness or badness. Each level of consciousness has advantages and disadvantages. They are good for different purposes.

Being in a higher consciousness does not make you more worthy than someone in a low consciousness. You are simply exploring different things. On the lower levels, there is a wider spectrum of experiences to explore. In 3D, you can explore struggle, drama, and defeat in all its forms. You can feel out of control and mystified by why things are happening. There's less room for that kind of exploration at 4D, and even less room at 5D. In that sense, 3D is better. Of course, most people tire of exploring negativity sooner than they tire of exploring happier experiences. So people tend to gravitate to 5D over time. In that sense, 5D is better. It just depends on what your goals are.

What does this have to do with manifesting? Well, manifesting in the 3D realm, with its slow, syrupy energy, is slow and obnoxious. It takes a long time, involves a lot of hard work, and has hit-or-miss results because there is so much opportunity for others' free will to interfere with your desires. When the energy around the topic of your desire is 3D energy, you can expect to have to push yourself into exhaustion, bully people into cooperation, and experience a lot of annoyances along the way. It makes the story of getting your desire a very long, drawn-out story of rags to (hopefully) riches...eventually....

The quickest way to get what you want is not dependent on Law of Attraction (LOA) techniques like visualization or affirmations. It's not dependent on how buzzed or bummed you feel. It's not dependent on how hard you think about what you want all day long.

It's dependent on how much of your energy around that topic is 3D, 4D, or 5D.

3D CONSCIOUSNESS

Choosing one kind of energy sets one chain of feelings, thoughts, actions, and results in motion. Choosing a different energy sets a different chain in motion. The areas of your life you have trouble with are probably mired in 3D energy. The areas of your life you have insight about but still some struggle are probably mostly 4D. And the areas that move smoothly, elegantly, and swiftly into what you love best are chock-full of 5D energy. To manifest what you want, you need to shift the energy around that topic into a higher vibration.

Although we can average out a person or planet's energy, calling it 3D, 4D, or 5D, in reality, you have different vibrational levels for different areas of your life. You may have a blissful 5D energy when you hold your newborn baby for the first time. You may have a crappy 3D energy when you do your taxes. You may have an inner-work-focused (4D) energetic state when you paint a picture, and then a stressed-out 3D energy when you try to sell it. It just depends.

But in the areas of life where you struggle the most, you've got 3D energy most of the time. How do I know that? Because 3D is the energy of delay, struggle, pain, disappointment, and fallen ice cream cones.

3D energy is dense and slow. It creates a significant time delay between the moment you intend something with your free will and the moment it manifests. In the space of that long delay, others on Planet Earth have a chance to add their two cents to your creation. That was part of the fun of coming to this world-- you knew you'd get to play with others, and we all agreed to allow ourselves and our creations to be affected by each other.

It's like we are painting our own pictures, while allowing our neighbors to slap on some paint when they feel like it. We paint a house and they add a pretty window. Cooperation is a very fun way to create.

Of course, on a planet of negativity, souls get confused about what is happening and how things work. That was part of the game, too. But it can be very frustrating to try and paint a house and discover that your neighbor has painted a monkey where you wanted a door. If you've forgotten that you agreed "we all can paint on each other's canvases," it gets very frustrating indeed!

In 3D consciousness, we think that what makes the world go round is *outward action* and *controlling others.* We spend our lives knocking on doors, keeping noses to the grindstone, pleading for help, insisting money will solve all problems, bullying our friends, and so on. 3D energy is the energy of struggle, micromanaging, and demanding. It emphasizes the need to protect ourselves.

In 3D, very little attention is paid to the psyche or the soul. If there is talk of the soul, it's emphasized that the soul needs to actively work in the world all the time, saving other souls by talking incessantly or building places of worship. In other words, at 3D, the "soul" just winds up being another thing that requires micromanaging and busy work.

I divide 3D consciousness into two kinds: lower and upper. The short version is, in lower 3D, nothing works very well and life stinks. In upper 3D, hard work gets you somewhere.

For each kind of consciousness (both in this chapter and the following chapters), I'll cover a few example topics: weight loss, career, finances, and relationships. These are just examples so you can see how the different densities (3D, 4D, and 5D) might contrast with one another.

Remember, you may have a very high level of consciousness in one area and a low one in another. That's okay. We are all exploring different parts of our lives in different ways.

Lower 3D Consciousness

At the lower end of 3D consciousness, you experience lots of struggle and lousy results. You rarely hear about any kind of easier path to getting what you want. On the rare times someone offers you one, it turns out to be a get-rich-quick scheme or a plan that's just unworkable in your life.

Since this consciousness is mired in struggle, it seems like the only way to get anywhere is to do something that feels uncomfortable. Those who stay in a "comfort zone" are belittled as weak, and people are encouraged to experience discomfort regularly.

Lower 3D energy is the slowest we can experience as human beings, and it's the most unpleasant. Though for other kinds of entities, low 3D energy is home and feels fine, to souls like ours, 3D is experienced as unpleasant negativity. It is the experience of judgyness and heavy limitations. We wanted to experiment with this experience, but now most of us human beings are finishing exploring lower 3D. We are "so over" our time in lower 3D and are ready to move up.

In lower 3D, your relationships with others tend to have a transactional nature. "You helped me, so I'll help you." "She makes me look good and I'm unlikely to do better at my age, so she can be my wife." You may act out of love for yourself or others occasionally, but most of your focus is on getting your basic needs met and getting ahead in life (or getting ahead in the afterlife, if you have a lower 3D consciousness about religion).

If you have lower 3D consciousness about a relationship, then you may have moments of love that spring out of you, but most of your focus is on how the other person can help you get ahead (or stay safe) socially or materially. For example, you may argue endlessly with your partner, but feel you have to stay with them because you don't know how to meet survival or social needs without them.

If you have lower 3D consciousness about weight loss, then you might work hard at dieting but nothing seems to help you lose weight.

If you have lower 3D energy around your career, you may work long hours at a crummy job and not get promoted or find anything better.

3D consciousness around finances might look like trying hard to save, but experiencing drama after drama that drains everything you try to save.

These are just examples. Lower 3D consciousness may turn up differently for you in your life. The key feature, though, remains "struggle that has lousy results."

Upper 3D Consciousness

All of the levels exist on a continuum, so there's bleed-over from every level to the next. In upper 3D consciousness, you've moved through some of the fear, powerlessness, and other negativity of this density and have healed a good deal of it, but remain enmeshed with a lot of negativity still. Here, the key feature is "struggle, but pretty good results."

For decades, self-help and motivational books focused on getting people from lower 3D to upper 3D. (Most writers had no idea they were doing this, but this was what was happening energetically.) This meant they were focusing on shifting self-talk to be more positive and action to be more proactive and responsibility-taking. These are interesting steps, but they don't shift a lot energetically, so it mostly landed people in upper 3D rather than someplace higher on the scale. The focus was on doing the hard work, staying positive, and appreciating the lovely results that came afterward.

When individuals moved from lower 3D to higher 3D, the idea of going through discomfort in order to get results became even more popular, since at this level of consciousness, good results can actually be had. "Get out of your comfort zone! Get into an unpleasant feeling forcing yourself to do new things, and you'll get success," became the standard advice.

People really do get good results from getting out of their comfort zone, at this level of consciousness. They really do get good results from just trying harder, putting in more hours, or being persistent in something unpleasant. It just requires a great deal of suffering!

Upper 3D challenged the transactional nature of relationships in lower 3D. They pointed out that treating people as a tit-for-tat way to fulfill needs ironically didn't fill our emotional needs!

Instead, upper 3D treats relationships as basically transactional, but as a trade in which you need to give more than they do or finagle a compromise that benefits both. "Give 80% and expect 20%." "Look for win/wins." This relieved a lot of burdens for friendships and partnerships, making it easier to get along with people, but it still meant a lot of work. Much of this work was in honing communication skills, doing helpful tasks for others that you don't necessarily enjoy, and being more polite. Again, struggle, but pretty good results.

People in 3D tend to work hard, and, unlike people in a lower 3D vibration, they get ahead. They work long hours, but they get that promotion. They struggle as entrepreneurs, but their company rises in income and comes out ahead. They study all night, but they get the A.

If you have upper 3D consciousness about weight loss, then you do lose weight and keep it off--but it takes a lot of vigilance and effort. You can't let up, and there's a struggle story.

If you have 3D consciousness about money, then you do slowly build up savings and wealth--it just takes a lot of stinginess and sacrifices. There's still a level of drama here. Happy endings, but drama.

Now that you know what 3D is like, check and see if your problem areas in life have any of this kind of energy. Is there an aspect of your life that feels like drudgery without results (lower 3D) or good results but full of struggle (upper 3D)? To manifest something better, the key is shifting the energy around the topic to be 5D. We'll go into how to do that in a later chapter. The first step is to understand where we're at and where we want to be, energetically.

What if the area of your life that you want to make better

isn't so bad as this? What if you've got less struggle, but still don't really have your dream? Let's turn to 4D consciousness, the in-between stage.

LOWER 4D CONSCIOUSNESS

We said that in 3D consciousness, what makes the world go round is *outward action* and *controlling others.* In 4D consciousness, we shift our vibration to one that is lighter, more loving, and more responsible. We've gotten tired of the endless hard work and struggle of trying to control the world around us in 3D, so we look for a better way.

In 4D, we think that what really creates change is *inward growth_*and *controlling ourselves.* In other words, we turn to self-help, psychology, shadow work, art therapy, yoga, Rolfing, meditation, and other modalities that will help us heal. We recognize how our wounds and mental filters have been affecting our reality, and we try to change them for the better. In the drudgery of 3D, we try to get what we want by acting out in the world. In 4D, we try to get what we want by healing, integrating, or improving our own minds, hearts, and bodies.

4D is a faster energy than 3D, so there is less opportunity for others to stick a finger in our pie with their free will. It still happens, but less often. Our desires are satisfied more often and more quickly in 4D. And although we may feel a pressure to "hurry up and become a better person," for the most part we have more happiness and a more relaxed attitude. Where 3D focuses on protection, 4D welcomes and explores vulnerability.

Spirituality changes as you move from 3D to 4D. In 3D, there is little emphasis on soulfulness. Instead, religion is a matter of the external world, where external sources tell you what the divine is like. Communication from the divine is filtered through other human beings--gurus, texts, or other external authorities.

In 4D, this shifts. Outer experience gives way to inner experience. Knowledge of the divine comes from within in 4D, and people begin to understand their own connection to it in their own way. They may still use labels like "God" or "Spirit," or they may perceive it as the universe, nature, angels, devas, common humanity, and so on.

4D is characterized by spiritual change (making the big transition from mostly fear-based 3D to mostly heart-centered 5D) and a new sensitivity to art, music, culture, and other forms of beauty as *transformative* experiences.

Now, of course people in every vibration can enjoy art and music. But at lower levels like 3D consciousness, art forms and beauty are perceived as frilly, nice-to-have things that don't matter much in the "real world." In 4D, we acknowledge that beauty in all its forms can actually *change* us as people. We may not understand exactly how it is that a movie or a song is able to shift our consciousness, our self-concept, and our vision of the world, but we acknowledge that it happens.

We make use of this by dwelling on stories that move us or decorating with objects that invite us to be different people. We tweak what we want by exploring characters and scenarios and by gathering inspiration from transformative ideals.

For example, if we want to become wealthier, we may explore archetypes of wealth in celebrities, icons, fictional characters, and Greek gods and goddesses. We may seek out fictional stories, tabloids (another kind of fiction, I suppose), and biographies to find out what wealthy lives might look like and how they might turn out.

Sometimes a story is a cautionary tale, warning us not to go overboard in one direction or another. Sometimes it is an inspiring tale. We explore to find out if the wealthy person we want to be looks more like Citizen Kane, Cleopatra, Walter White, Oprah Winfrey, or Scrooge McDuck. By engaging with stories and the lives of other people, we refine our dreams and connect to new energies.

People in 3D get fascinated by stories, too, but they usually see them as wishful thinking or idle daydreams. In 4D, we acknowledge the transformative power these stories have in our lives through the experience shared and the beauty that inspires.

Later, in 5D, we see that transformation can happen even without the experience of beauty or stories, and we're not as fixated on transformation anyway because we're very much enjoying our 5D experiences and much more comfortable living from our true selves. We may still have transformations at 5D, but it's not so engrossing as the shift from the fearfulness of 3D to the heart-centeredness in 5D. According to Sara Landon (and the Council she channels), 4D is a transition stage of transformation and healing. 4D is all about this shift from 3D fearfulness and control to 5D heart-centeredness and play.

In this book, I won't say much about tools for entering 4D, mainly because there are just so many good books and techniques already out there. There are so many ways to familiarize yourself with what patterns you have in your thinking, feeling, and body awareness. Psychotherapy, art therapy, bodywork, yoga, hypnotherapy, EMDR, tapping, psychic ability, inner child work--the list is almost endless of techniques that can help you better understand the results in thought, feeling, and body that you are getting. Though I won't be discussing these in-depth, I don't want to give the impression that getting to 4D is unimportant. Though it's possible to move quickly from 3D to 5D, a grounding in 4D energy is what keeps us from slipping too far too fast from our 5D highs.

Although it sounds nice to be in 5D all the time, the reality is, our energetic awareness is bound to slip, and we're bound to choose a lower-vibrational energy at some point. Unless you're a spiritual master, you're just not going to be aware of what you're doing with energy all the time. If we have spent enough time in 4D to build familiarity with our mental, emotional, and physical patterns, then when we slip from 5D energy, we don't have to wait for crises in order to know our energy has drifted.

Instead, we may notice that we are falling back into old habits of thinking or old emotional baggage. That then alerts us that our energy must have gone off-kilter, and we can return to energetic awareness and choose 5D again. If you've attuned to 4D energy in the past, you may recognize old slips. "Hey, I'm comparing myself to all the men around me again, just like I compared myself with my brother so much when we were kids. Something's up. Let me check my energy." Then you don't have to wait for big 3D problems to arise to let you know you drifted energetically. You don't have to wait for a big, blow-up argument with the boss who reminds you of your brother. You drop into 4D, rather than falling all the way into crummy 3D problems. 4D serves as a transition space, not only for rising into 5D, but also for catching ourselves before we go too deep back into 3D.

I divide the 4D level of consciousness into a lower and higher version.

Lower 4D Consciousness

The hallmark of lower 4D consciousness is huge improvements coming from personal growth work. In lower 4D, you get a big bang for your buck on personal growth work. You've moved out of 3D, where you thought the only thing that mattered was changing what's around you and doing a little positive self-talk. In lower 4D, you start doing deeper inner work and reaping big benefits from it. You get energy healing, you go to therapy, you befriend your inner child. You heal old wounds and embrace parts of your shadow. You get in touch with your body. You figure out how past experiences have shaped the way you think and feel.

And the results you get from this are typically big. You might see sweeping changes in your circumstances as a result of this work, though usually there are some "holdout" parts of your life that stay stuck in 3D. Even if not much changes on the outside, you experience a much higher quality of life within.

People in lower 4D may still subscribe to the "get out of your comfort zone" advice, but they do try and make the discomfort as minimal as possible. They still don't envision a world in which new things can feel good and comfortable, but they are less bullying to themselves about *how* they try new things.

For example, they may assume going on a blind date has to feel uncomfortable, but will try to reduce the discomfort a little by inviting friends to double date with them. They may tweak their daily processes to be a little more comfortable and inspiring, maybe by adding music, working from home, working outside, decorating their workspace, or finding some other small way to make "doing the thing" a little more pleasant.

In relationships, there's a 4D acknowledgement that people genuinely change, and that our constant change will upset any transactional trade-offs we were trying to make in 3D. When you've experienced, say, a movie that shifts how you think of yourself, it shifts how you see the people around you and how you want to act in the world. And when you realize you can change so much, you realize it's unrealistic to expect everyone else to stay the same.

For example, you may realize it's unrealistic to expect Great-Aunt Harriet to bring sweet potato pie for every Christmas dinner or your sister to always be the control freak. You realize they may be changing just as much and wanting to reinvent themselves.

You realize past transactions ("At family get-togethers, I'll bring cheerfulness and make a lot of jokes to liven things up, and my sister will take care of the food and the dishes") are too limiting to everyone involved. Instead, your interactions become more like flexible negotiations, gently making room for whatever shifts happen in you or the others involved.

It's also common in 4D to discover that you want to hang out with an entirely different kind of person than you did in 3D. You make new friendships. Some old friendships peter out, or you tweak them so that you don't see those people as often, or only under conditions you're more comfortable with.

If you have lower 4D consciousness about weight loss, then you may find a diet or exercise plan you're okay with, and then tweak it in a self-expressive way. You buy really snazzy containers for your salads, or you play your favorite music while you jog. There's still effort involved--it's not a breeze--but you've found some ways to include your own ideas of beauty or inspiration. You may explore your childhood associations with food and love and do inner work on that as well. You may find a movement technique that helps you get in touch with your body.

If you have 4D consciousness about your career, you may have changed to a different company, one where the people are a little nicer and the atmosphere is more relaxed. You're still doing the same thing, but you're beginning to satisfy some of the needs of the heart in the details. You may explore how your family of origin thought about career, and how that has affected you. With such new focus on your internal experience, you may discover you've been working in the wrong field, or for the wrong reasons. You might now know what you'd like to do but feel a big gap between moving from where you are now (inner insight) to where you want to be (new external career).

4D consciousness tweaks about finances might look like a cool new savings app that takes a bit of the sting out of saving, or being open to investing in a cause that inspires you (while still engaging in "doing the thing"--checking credentials, handling paperwork, doing due diligence about the organization). There's still a feeling of effort, but also enjoyment. 4D inner work might show you what money represents to you, how much money you think it is "okay" to possess, and how your ideas about rich people affect what you can do with money.

Lower 4D involves big gains from personal growth and minor gains from tweaking your activities to include a little beauty or creativity.

UPPER 4D CONSCIOUSNESS

The big differences between upper 4D and lower 4D involve how much struggle you are willing to put up with, and how much (or how little) benefit you get from inner self-improvement work.

In upper 4D consciousness, activities that feel like struggle begin to stand out in an unpleasant way. You can't say that things are objectively worse than before--it's not that you're losing money, or you're putting the weight back on, or whatever. It's just that some of the activities you used to be able to make yourself do now feel like too much drama and struggle.

If you try to go back to the old weight-loss method you did in upper 3D, it just feels like way too much work. You wonder how you ever made yourself do that.

You can't get yourself to work the long hours in your career that you drudged through back in 3D. It just seems like misery.

"Struggle" options now feel much more unpleasant, because you're experimented with slightly improving options and finding things that don't feel as bad. It's not like life is a cakewalk now, but things are better. Going back to the old way now seems deeply unpleasant. You may call yourself "lazy" because you don't have the patience to put up with the drudgery you routinely endured in 3D or lower 4D.

The other thing that differentiates upper 4D from lower 4D is that you no longer get great results from inner self-improvement work. You hit a block, and inner work just doesn't seem to do much anymore. The last few problems in your life don't seem to budge, no matter how many therapy sessions or Reiki treatments you get. You try to more deeply understand your past, your inner child, your neurolinguistics, and so on-- and yet, deeper understanding just doesn't seem to help create change anymore. You can't seem to control yourself enough to get what you want, and you're not sure you even want to, because the struggle involved seems too unpleasant and unnecessary now.

In relationships in upper 4D, there's more of an emphasis on building from love rather than fear. Relationships that are fear-based often become very, very frustrating and annoying at this stage.

You find you just cannot put up with the low vibrational garbage spewed at you from Crazy Cousin Earl, and you have a crisis of conscience about whether you can end the relationship or not. Fear-based beliefs like, "I need to stay on good terms with this person because I may be down-and-out someday and need them to take me in" or "I have to put up with toxic behavior because we're biologically related" come up to be challenged.

At 4D, you have higher energy, but you may find it difficult to keep it steady when deeply engaged with people in very low vibrations, and you may need space until you stabilize your vibration. Since you may not be ready to let go of all fear yet, you may strike a compromise. "I'll hang out with Crazy Cousin Earl, but only at Christmas, and if he starts talking racist, I'm going to tell him to stop and leave if he doesn't."

The Lower 4D Trap

It's common for people to get stuck in what I call "the Lower 4D Trap." As I've said, when you first enter lower 4D, you get a big boost in your life: crazy-good personal growth from inner work. The first time people encounter the idea that their thoughts and feelings are powerful, it's a rush! Often we experience some mind-blowing insights when we first begin this kind of work, and our lives shift radically for the better. We hunger for the next big insight to shift our lives further.

The trouble is, big mental insights are part of the realm of lower 4D, and become less common as we rise in vibration. If you become attached to startling mental "aha"s as proof of spiritual growth, then you keep cycling in 4D endlessly, trying to find the next big insight again and again and feeling puzzled why your life isn't changing much anymore. The first few self-help books or woo-woo seminars produced life-changing results. But as you energetically shift from lower 4D to upper 4D, those inner-work-centered methods seem to give less and less bang for their buck...

Often people in 4D fall in love with the easy, transformative insights they had in lower 4D, and they don't want to let that go. Instead of acknowledging that more seminars, more therapy, and more self-help books are not going to move the needle, they seek out more and more in the hope that one big insight will shift their outer experience the way it did in lower 4D.

This problem is intensified for the many, many spiritual seekers who spent childhood and young adulthood in 3D energy and then had a huge blossoming moment when their life shifted into 4D. Because many of us have spent hundreds or even thousands of lifetimes in 3D, the shift into 4D felt like-- and perhaps was--the biggest experience ever. It was natural to assume that all big spiritual shifts would be similar--very dramatic mental insights.

For those who arrived on Planet Earth with their vibrations already in 4D, clinging to mental insights as the ultimate spiritual experience is not as attractive, but even they can get stuck if they become "insight junkies" rather than letting spiritual experience evolve.

In lower 4D, insights create massive change. In upper 4D, though, insights do not happen as often because insights are usually mind-based. Upper 4D is moving towards 5D, which is heart-based. A huge mental perspective shift is characteristic in lower 4D, where the mind is the powerhouse. In the higher realms, the mind is an assistant, not the prime director. The heart is the field of change there.

When there's a shift in the heart, it rarely feels like a mental insight. Instead, it's experienced as an energetic shift that, put into words, sounds very simple. The heart might say, "Actually, I *love* this thing I'm doing," or "Meh, not for me." It does not usually sound very deep, intellectually.

For those who really enjoy the life of the mind, it can be disappointing to release the complex, deep "aha" moments of lower 4D and move into the simpler (but usually more joyous) shifts of the heart that are emerging in upper 4D and strengthen in 5D.

There's just not a big, complicated story about why you shift from one activity, relationship, or state of being to another in 5D. While in 4D, you might have had a powerful "aha" moment that, for example, all your life you've been craving the attention of your absent father, and that every boss has been a stand-in for him, and that's why you have a complicated relationship with authority, and you're coming to terms with your inner masculine figure and that's why you want to become an entrepreneur and re-parent yourself...in 5D, there are no such complicated explanations of why you make new choices. In 5D, it's just an energetic pull of aliveness, spaciousness, freedom (or whatever your sense of 5D energy is).

In 5D, there's no detailed story of why you did what you did and why you're doing something different from now on. Partly this is because there is no judgyness, so there's no need to describe in detail what was "wrong." Partly this is because there is more freedom in 5D, so there's no need to justify why you want a new direction. You're free to do whatever you choose, no justification necessary.

When you shift from lower 4D to upper 4D, you may find yourself being given the same, seemingly bland 5D advice over and over: "Consult your intuition and take baby steps" or "Listen to your heart" or "Take better care of yourself" or "You do you."

No matter how many bodywork masters or psychics you visit, you may keep getting thrown back onto yourself, being told the next step has to come from within. If you're still hunting for a mind-based insight, this can be maddening! Mind-based insights have their place, but as you make the transition from 4D to 5D, you are being asked to ground more and more into your own energy and your own heart.

You may long for an insight about discovering yet another hidden belief, past-life memory, or trapped trauma in your spine. But cycling endlessly in the quest for more inner work will not move you forward at this point. At upper 4D, the way forward is to move into the heart and let an *energetic* pull guide you rather than a mental insight.

Am I Stuck in 3D or 4D?

You might wonder, "Hey, if my manifestations aren't working out very well, how do I know if this area is stuck in 3D or in 4D?"

The answer is, in 3D, you will feel tempted to jump in and take outward action over and over, trying to solve the problem. In 4D, you will feel tempted to do more inner work over and over, trying to solve the problem.

For example, if you want a new house and can't seem to find one you like that you can afford, is your temptation to call realtor after realtor, bank after bank? Or is it to do yet another Tarot reading, yet another chat with your inner child?

Of course, you can have a mix of vibrations, and people can have impulses for more than one kind of thing, but if there's more of a slant towards outer action, it's 3D, and if it's more of a slant toward inner action, it's 4D.

Practicing Heart-Based Choices

Since the old 3D ways feel too hard now, people in upper 4D consciousness usually either continue an option they feel fairly neutral about (perhaps tweaking it with a few inspiring features) or experiment with trying a heart-based choice.

Heart-based choices are decisions made from pure love,

pure joy. It's not the emotions, per se, but the very high energy underneath that makes choices heart-based.

These choices feel like fun, and although you may have a goal in mind, the process is as exciting as the goal. Heart-based choices are based in the energy and intention of play, joy, and love, rather than trying to "get somewhere" or "fix something" or "be a good person."

In 5D, heart-based choices are the norm. In upper 4D, people begin experimenting with heart-based choice, but they usually get mixed results. They are not yet energetically in the place where heart-based choices flow easily and well. Still, the practice helps them move more towards 5D.

Now we've looked at the kinds of energy in which your problem areas are likely stuck. The thing you want to change in your life might be mired in lower 3D (lots of struggle, lousy results), upper 3D (lots of struggle, good results), lower 4D (new insights, things are much better than they were but not ideal), or upper 4D (trying out choosing from the heart, things are good but you haven't quite gotten where you wanted to be). You don't have to know exactly what level of energy you have in order to shift it, but it helps to have a general idea.

So if 5D consciousness is great for lining up our manifestations, what does that even look like? Let's turn to 5D consciousness (and higher!).

LOWER 5D CONSCIOUSNESS

5D is a realm of bliss, ease, and love. Although not everything is perfect, things are a lot smoother and more enjoyable here.

According to Matt Kahn, at low levels of consciousness, we begin to learn that physical stuff won't fulfill us, but we still think spiritual accomplishments will. At higher levels, we realize that fulfillment is an energy frequency that depends on intention, not accomplishments. 5D is an energy level that focuses not on outward action nor mental or emotional "work," but rather just the experience and intention of love.

Although I'll call it "love" or "joy" here, really the experience of 5D energy feels different to different people. On an emotional level, it may feel more like power, freedom, beauty, connection, ease, magic, or something else.

You create through joy in 5D, not to improve yourself or fix your life. Instead of saying, "My life is not good enough; I need to make it better," the attitude is more "What would be fun right now? How could this area of my life be even more enjoyable?"

Noticing a "problem" and taking action is not about worthiness anymore. It's just about noticing what you'd enjoy more and doing that. Both the results and the process feel good. You still take action and do inner work in 5D, but not because you think it's going to change your life. You do it for fun. And if an action or a method of inner work doesn't feel enjoyable, you don't do it because you know there's a better way.

At 5D consciousness, you acknowledge that if a process or activity is not enjoyable, it's not going to work. I don't just mean that you won't put up with crummy activities. I mean that at this level, the *results* from actions that feel crummy are crummy, too! Bullying yourself to do something you dislike never turns out well, at this level of consciousness. (At upper 3D, bullying works all the time! See why it matters what kind of energy you have?)

At 5D consciousness, you have healed a lot of the fear that said that if you don't "blah blah blah" like society says, you'll crash and burn. Now you make heart-based choices regularly. Doing something new doesn't take you out of your comfort zone. New things don't feel uncomfortable; they just feel strange.

In 5D, you may occasionally slip back into choosing fear or limitation over what your heart is telling you, but since the results tend to stink, you swing back to heart-centeredness quickly.

Heart-based choices don't feel like effort--at least, not in any bad sense. You may be expending physical or mental energy, but you don't feel drained on an energetic level. In a 5D choice, you may give up something--money, time, effort, and so on-- but what you give up does not feel like a hardship or a problem. 5D choices will never involve any sacrifice that bothers you. It is like when you joyfully hand money over for something you really want that is on sale--it cost you something, technically, but there is no feeling that it cost you anything worth bothering about.

Consider a tennis player who loves her sport. She's breathing hard, running around, swatting tennis balls--clearly, there's some physical "effort"--but when she is in the zone, she just loves everything she's doing. She may feel physically tired after the game and need a nap, but her spirits are flush with energy even as she plumps her pillow. In 5D, more and more of your activities take on this effortless nature. The activities are spiritually renewing and rewarding, both in their results, and as you're doing them. It's work that feels like play, healthy food that feels like indulgence, or auto repair that feels like doing a fun puzzle.

At 5D, you don't often come across people who rub you the wrong way, and relationships get a lot easier. Sometimes you notice a person in 3D doing things that used to make you feel judgy, but now a lot of the judgyness has left you. Now you see the same behavior with amusement, compassion, or neutrality.

You know that all beings are made of love and worthy of love, *and* you also know that there's no reason to force yourself to spend time with someone who doesn't resonate with you.

When you truly, deeply know that all beings are equally worthy, it takes a lot of the drama out of choosing who to be with. In 3D and 4D, you might have felt conflicted at such moments. "I really don't like Susan, but I know she's just as good as anyone. Maybe I should force myself to hang out with her until I like her." There's an inkling of doubt that you really believe Susan is worthy, and you have to "prove" you do by hanging out with her and trying to find something to like. In 5D, there's no doubt. Of course Susan is worthy, and so there's no need to prove it by hanging out with her. If she doesn't resonate with you, that's no judgment on her or you. You simply move on to someone who does.

If you have 5D consciousness about weight loss, then your focus has probably shifted from seeing your body as less-than to just wanting to enjoy having a body. You may have discovered-- or more likely, created through a process of experimenting-- a diet or exercise plan that you find both enjoyable and manageable. There's an ease and flow to your process. When there are hiccups, you don't take it personally or blame yourself. You just make some new shifts to your process to adapt. Whatever you do, you notice how it feels, and you make sure every step of your plan is something you can genuinely enjoy in the moment.

5D at work means heart-based choices are the norm. You're doing mostly tasks you enjoy and you have a broad idea of how your work makes the world happier, more relaxed, healthier, safer, more respectful, or some other goal that speaks to your heart. Occasionally you may do things that feel neutral to you, and even less often you may find yourself bullying yourself into doing something you dislike. But that happens less and less often on this continuum.

For finances, 5D consciousness may involve spontaneous increases in wealth, investments in organizations you really resonate with, and other financial improvements *that require very little upkeep, or only upkeep you usually enjoy.* When hiccups occur, you listen to your heart and make adjustments, and soon the flow starts again.

5D does not mean perfect health, wealth, or relationships. There will still be problems, and sometimes even drama. But the overall level of effort needed is much less, and the overall results from heart-based choices tend to be very good. (The overall results from fear-based choices will be much worse in 5D than in 4D or 3D. Those choices will just not fit with anything else in your life, and will invite struggle and drama back into the area you make such choices in.)

In lower 5D, life isn't perfect, but it's good enough that you begin to trust in a new relationship to happiness. You start to see that change is worth the risk. As my guides put it:

You develop a different relationship to happiness and it becomes more important than avoiding fear. Avoiding fear is not the same thing as seeking happiness. Avoiding fear usually involves avoiding risks and taking the dull, mildly painful route in all things. Seeking happiness risks the experience of fear, but will not settle for what is dull and painful...To choose more happiness, you must be willing to say "no" to small hurts that seem safe and "yes" to big joys that seem risky.

In lower 5D, you may still have some fear to face occasionally in your pursuit of wonderful things. In middle 5D, the fears involved in risk become less relevant, because you have even more trust and even higher energy. Let's turn our attention to middle 5D next.

MIDDLE 5D CONSCIOUSNESS

The gradations of 5D are still somewhat mysterious to me. I'm not sure if I know many people in upper 5D, so I'll confine this discussion to the mid-range. We need more mavericks exploring and explaining the upper regions, so if you know anything about upper 5D, please share!

There are two main differences between lower 5D and middle 5D. The first is a difference in what we look for. In lower 5D, your focus tends to be on finding something that feels high-vibrational. In middle 5D, your focus is on finding what resonates with you personally.

The second difference is in how we interact with lower vibrations. In lower 5D, we're very careful to avoid low vibrations because they feel bad and drag us down. In middle 5D, our own vibration is strong enough that we tend to shift the low vibrations we encounter.

Let's look at these two differences more closely.

Middle 5D Shifts Us from Hunting High Vibes to Hunting What Hits the Spot for Us

At lower 5D, life is finally getting easy. Things feel good, people get along, and there's relief from fear, sadness, and anger. Because you've moved up from regions with a lot more negativity, at first, lower 5D just feels heavenly. You're so grateful that things are working out that you're not very choosy about how your joy, ease, and comfort play out. You're just glad you're getting some!

Once you've adjusted and integrated more 5D energy, you begin to realize that some joyful energies feel different from others. Some are more satisfying than others. Some kind, loving, high-vibrational people feel absolutely fabulous to you, while others feel fine but not...exciting.

This is a very confusing moment for many people. You spent all that time in deep negativity, and now your life is finally shaping up into ease and friendly people. At first you just feel thrilled to be in a happy life at last. With time, you realize your life could be a little more happy or a little less happy, depending on how you direct your energies and who you hang out with.

The reason this feels confusing is because you can tell all these 5D options are still *good.* They're still high-vibrational. Anything 5D feels a lot better than lower vibes. There's more joy, love, honesty, kindness, and so on without effort at this level. It's not like the options seem poor, scummy, dingy, angry, or otherwise unpleasant, and that's why you're getting picky. They're still all really good options. It's just that some don't "hit the spot" the way others do.

For example, suppose Felicia has been living a 4D life. She's had some insights about how her thoughts affect the way her life turns out, but she still has a lot of problems. For one thing, she can't find any kind of movement she likes, and her friends all seem to drag her down. As Felicia works on getting in touch with 5D energy, she winds up discovering a yoga class that she loves. The movement helps her body, the class is low-key and peaceful, and all the people in her class are welcoming and high-vibrational. At the lower 5D level, Felicia is just thrilled she's finally found something she likes! She's so happy that her new friends are so supportive and have such great energy about them.

As Felicia integrates 5D energy and moves upward into middle 5D, though, she begins to notice that the yoga class--while still being enjoyable--doesn't quite "hit the spot."

This is confusing to Felicia. Before, she didn't even realize she had a spot to hit! And the new friends in her yoga class are just as kind as ever; they haven't changed. They're not toxic people. They're still obviously high-vibrational.

It's hard for Felicia to say good-bye and look for something more, given that the yoga class and the people in it are fine. In fact, they're better than anything she had before! Felicia hesitates to look for something new. Shouldn't she just be satisfied with this mild happiness, given that it's so much better than anything she had before?

In other words, as you or Felicia or anyone moves into 5D, we are confronted with some puzzling ideas:

- Just because some activity, person, or place is high-vibrational does not mean it's best for us, personally.
- You can acknowledge that something or someone is very high-vibrational, and yet not want to be around it or them so much. Not because they're unpleasant--they're not; nothing in 5D is actually unpleasant--but because you sense there's something out there that's more your thing.
- Ironically, as you move higher and higher in vibration, you become less concerned about whether things are "high-vibrational," and more concerned about whether they fit *your* vibration.

Let's try a different example: your favorite horror movie. When you're in 3D, you might enjoy getting scared because it's a novel experience. You sort of want to know the ins and outs of how it feels in your body, how you react afterwards, and how you bond with your friends in sharing a fearful experience.

As you move to 4D in the area of horror films, you might become interested in why this particular film appeals to you psychologically. Maybe you explore why dark, claustrophobic places scare you and heights don't, or vice versa. Maybe you analyze the characters in the movie, figuring out who they might represent in your life, or maybe you dive deep into the themes and what they might mean about your soul path.

At lower 5D, you notice all the fear vibrations a lot more and find them uncomfortable. You realize you could watch a movie with a lot higher vibrations, so you go do that instead.

At middle 5D, your relationship to the old favorite film may shift again. Although you may still dislike the fear aspect, you may recognize something in the movie that feels like "you." There's something about it that hits the spot. You begin to watch it again. Somehow, you find it easy to overlook the fear aspect of the film and just home in on the energy in the movie that does resonate with you. You may continue to watch the movie, just not noticing or being bothered much by the parts intended to scare you. Or you may eventually drift into finding a different movie that includes the parts that "hit the spot" while not being so fearful. Either way, the transition happens pretty naturally.

In Middle 5D, We Become Less Entangled with Lower Vibrations

The horror movie example brings us to the other (though related) difference: in lower 5D, we try to avoid low vibrations, but in middle 5D, we don't need to expend effort avoiding them as often.

There will still be moments when you reject something because it has a lower state of energy, of course. There will always be times when we recognize an energy state that isn't good for what we want and pass it by. But at middle 5D, it doesn't take as much planning and action to do this.

For one thing, having higher vibrations in an area of life means that lower-vibration options don't seem as relevant anymore. You don't have to make studied, conscious choices to avoid them; you barely notice they were options at all! Intellectually, you may know it's an option, but it doesn't feel relevant.

It's like going through a checkout line in a store. Intellectually, you know you could grab an item off the shelf and whack the cashier with it. But for most of us, we never even consider doing that. It's off our radar. And if it does come into our mind as a stray thought, it's pretty easy to dismiss that low-vibrational choice. It's so clearly not what we want (or what the cashier wants).

So at middle 5D, although you still have the choice to dip yourself into some shady or unpleasant vibrations, you don't pay a lot of attention to those options and it's not a struggle to avoid them. Contrast this with lower 5D. At lower 5D, we often still feel the effect of a lifetime of habits that put us into lower vibrations, and some of those choices feel relevant because it's what we used to do or what we still feel tempted by old patterns to do. We know Cousin Earl's conversations are toxic, but we spent fifteen years enduring them because "that's what a good cousin does." Now we're trying to jettison that old choice and do something that feels more loving and higher-vibrational to ourselves. It takes a little effort to make the wiser choice.

There's another reason why middle 5D entangles us less with lower vibrations: we can shift them better. The higher your vibration, the easier it is to shift the energy around you to resonate.

You do this unconsciously and naturally at every moment, no matter what vibrational level you're at--but when you're at middle 5D, you've got a heck of a lot of energetic power, so the effects you cause are stronger. Mean people may drop some of their mean behavior while they're around you, because the mean options don't seem as relevant to them in your energetic space. Haunted houses may get a little cheerier when you stroll in. Buggy computers may process a little faster and smoother.

Over time, you start to notice that even "low-vibrational" stuff seems to get better when you're present, so you don't worry so much about encountering it. That doesn't mean you start visiting war-torn countries for your vacation or anything, but you worry less about whether the environment you're about to enter is "high-vibrational" or not. You're just interested in whether it resonates with you or not.

Sometimes, following what resonates brings you into super-happy, shining houses of the highest dimensional quality. Other times, following what resonates brings you into a dingy

3D house of squalor because it's fun to shift the energy of it. Either way, it becomes less of a conscious calculation of "What is high-vibrational?" and more of an instinctive "What feels fun? What feels like me today?"

SPECULATIONS ABOUT UPPER 5D AND BEYOND

I don't think I actually know anyone higher than 5D, so this chapter is speculation. As always, take what resonates and leave the rest.

Higher Vibrations Gradually Shift Everything

With every level, the highest vibrations we are engaging with tend to slowly affect other areas of our lives.

For example, if a person has 3D energy in every area, and then begins to have 4D energy about their love life, then that 4D energy will slowly edge into other parts of their life. Becoming aware of one aspect of their inner mind in relationships would help them become slightly more aware of other patterns in career, finances, health, and so on.

4D energy moves very slowly--faster than 3D, of course, but still taking decades or even lifetimes to spread throughout a person's entire life if no effort is made to speed things up.

5D energy gradually spreads throughout your life, as well, but a little faster. Once you have heart-based 5D energy around gardening, for example, other parts of your life will begin to pop into that energy. Again, it may take years, but it will filter through your life even without any effort on your part.

I speculate that at even higher levels--6D, or perhaps 7D-- all lower levels of your life are healed and raised spontaneously, even those that seem unrelated to us at 4 or 5D. This is because the energy frequencies of 6D and 7D are much, much more powerful and much, much faster.

At that level, you see how the various parts of your life are all connected at a deep level. Sensing that powerful energy in one area immediately illuminates it everywhere in your life. There is such connection and unity among the parts of your life that they instantly heal, whereas in 5D it still takes some time to heal.

I do not know anyone at 6D or 7D, and I do not even know if someone at that vibration can embody on a planet like Earth. It may be an energy that can't slow down enough to form a physical body as we know it. This is just what I speculate about these higher energies.

Stay in Your Comfort Zone

Here's another speculation about higher energies: at higher levels, we no longer grow through pain or discomfort.

At 3D, we have sayings like, "No pain, no gain." The idea is that any kind of positive change requires a lot of suffering.

At 4D, we move into the idea of "get out of your comfort zone." Again, the idea is that change requires some kind of unpleasantness. When the unpleasant feelings are mild, we call it discomfort. When the unpleasant feelings are intense, we call it pain. Either way, in 3D and 4D, supposedly the only way we can experience new energies is to feel something unpleasant.

For most people, "comfort zone" has become synonymous with "the area in which you are not growing." They can't imagine that growth could happen in a state of comfort--that you could be developing as a person, AND feeling great (or even just neutral) doing it. This idea that a comfort zone is a zone of stagnation is built on a lie:

New things always mean unpleasant feelings and sensations (i.e. discomfort).

The truth is something slightly, but meaningfully different:

*New things always mean **strange** feelings and sensations.*

Strange feelings may be pleasant, unpleasant, or neutral. At 3D, the strange feelings are often very unpleasant! At 4D, they are usually mildly unpleasant. But often at 5D, and all the time at higher levels, new things don't require feeling bad. You don't have to leave your comfort zone to grow. You can encounter new experiences and just feel neutral, or even good.

As we Ascend to 5D and beyond, we are moving into a new spiritual paradigm, one where growth happens in joy--without pain, lousy feelings, discomfort, and other forms of unpleasantness. We ditch the "no discomfort, no growth" paradigm and align with a new one: "growth involves encountering the unfamiliar, so it will feel strange, but not necessarily uncomfortable." Or, a little pithier, "Strange can feel good."

Really, as kids, we often already know that experiencing new things doesn't have to involve discomfort. I've seen lots of little kids take their first bite of cake ever, and none of them looked the slightest bit uncomfortable about it. It's weird for them, but pleasant.

And often I'll see some kid do something that seems much more dramatically new, and it's not even "a thing" for them. Some kids are gifted singers, and they just break into song in the middle of a group of people, performing before strangers for the first time. "Hey, kid, wasn't that uncomfortable? You've never done that before. Heck, I'd be scared to sing in front of strangers." And many of them say, "That wasn't uncomfortable. I loved it." It may have been a stretch for them, but the sensations that came up weren't sensations of discomfort. Those stretching feelings just felt good. They were doing something quite new--*while staying in a state of comfort.*

As you explore new things in 5D (and higher), pretend you are Alice in Wonderland or an explorer of a strange new world. You'd expect there to be unfamiliar things all around, but the unfamiliarity would feel exciting, intriguing, mystifying, or just odd. Curiouser and curiouser!

If you notice, tons and tons of children's tales hold the motif of encountering a strange (but not bad-feeling) person or place. Places and people in certain children's books may appear wild, woolly, bizarre, or outlandish, but the main characters discovering them are often delighted rather than uncomfortable. (There are lots of stories and scenes about uncomfortable strangeness, too, of course, but those won't help you get used to the new paradigm. Be selective.) What if you met a unicorn today? It would be strange, certainly, but probably not uncomfortable. (Perhaps it depends on the unicorn.)

If it helps, consider how growth happens in a heavenly place or the Other Side. At 6D, 7D, or higher, do you really think angels are groaning, "Oh, I'm growing as an angel, which means I've got to feel discomfort here in this land of bliss"?

Most of us acknowledge that at some point, in some otherworldly place, creatures grow through joy rather than discomfort. If you believe that, then why couldn't we experience more growth through joy here on Earth? Maybe we won't get to nonstop joy all the time here, but we can experience new things with less discomfort at least. That's a common evolution as we move into 5D.

Growing means making unfamiliar states of being into familiar ones. It's about choosing which new experiences you want to have and be, and then bringing those into your life and making them familiar, easy-to-access, or easy-to-understand experiences.

So long as you are reaching into the unfamiliar and making it familiar, you are growing, whether it involves discomfort, neutrality, or joy. At 5D, our unfamiliar experiences begin to become more and more joyful. We stay in comfort more and more as we explore. I suspect that at even higher levels, the unfamiliar is always (or nearly always) joyful. There, there's no such thing as stepping out of your comfort zone, because everything new is merely strange, not uncomfortable.

If you are at 6D or 7D, or know someone who is, I invite you to explore and share. There is still much to discover and explain about consciousness.

RESISTANT ENERGY

Now that we've talked about many levels of consciousness, what exactly is resistance?

Resistance is energy that slows movement and manifestation. It keeps you from getting what you want too quickly.

On the Other Side, the cosmos sorts itself automatically. If you discover some energy that resonates with you on the Other Side, you can move toward it without delay.

Whatever doesn't resonate, you can move away from, again with no delay. Everything finds harmony without effort. Higher dimensions allow free movement, and you easily find and gravitate towards that which resonates with you.

Lower-vibrational energies like 3D and 4D are different. They were created for new experiences. Specifically, they help slow movement down. They help us explore energies that don't resonate with us--stuff that we feel aversion to.

3D and 4D energy are serving us. They help create a gap between our wanting something and our getting it. This gap is what makes a story, a life experience. Low-vibrational energy is the universe's method for creating a story of moving from not having to having, or for exploring negativity.

Low-vibrational energy keeps us from sorting the universe into "what resonates" and "what doesn't resonate" so fast. On the Other Side, that sorting happens so quickly and so easily that you don't even notice it. You find what resonates and let go of what doesn't with ease. Exploration is a whirl of fun, zooming quickly to whatever floats your boat and easily dropping whatever sinks it.

On Planet Earth, the low-vibrational energy slows the sorting. It creates a forced union between you and stuff that doesn't resonate. It creates a forced separation between you and what <u>does</u> resonate. As you attune energy, you slowly move towards what you want, but it takes a while and may be rocky. That time period of seeking is the entertaining story of life.

Resistant 3D and 4D energy makes those stories of rags-to-riches and ups-and-downs possible. They are there to help us.

Because 3D and 4D energies are just here to help us, we can let them know when their job is done. When you get tired of the gap between wanting something and getting it, you can let those slow, resistant energies know you're finished with that game. You give that energy permission to let go and dissolve.

Easier said than done, right? How are we supposed to let resistant energy know that it's no longer needed?

You may have already explored dozens of practices designed to help you let go of stuck, resistant energy. Maybe you've tried the Sedona Method, or psychotherapy, or primal screaming, or eye movement reprocessing. Maybe you've tried prayer, meditation, or Reiki.

All of these practices are really just permission slips we give to ourselves. The choice to allow old, stuck, resistant energy to dissolve is always available to us, but most of the time we don't think it's realistic to actually let it go. Then we devise a complicated procedure for letting low-vibrational energy go. If it's complicated and takes a long time, then sometimes we feel we have better permission to let it go. "I 'did the work,'" we tell our friends. "It must be okay for that low-vibe stuff to go now, because I kept doing this practice hard-core for months."

If we encounter a guru or other person who really, really impresses us, sometimes we give ourselves permission to have a better life then, without a lot of hard work. On an energetic level, we notice what energetic choice the master is making. We sense, deep down, how they are letting go of resistance, and then we copy that (usually unconsciously) in our own way.

So if you can meet one of your spiritual heroes, sometimes

that helps you release a lot of resistance. But again, that's mostly just you giving yourself permission to let the junk go. You get a boost from seeing which choices they are making, but in the end it's you choosing to let 3D or 4D energy know its job is done.

Choosing to let resistant energy go is fundamentally just a choice, but it doesn't seem that easy when you're mired in lower-vibrational energy. When you're deep in resistance, resistance tells you, "You can let us go, but it's very, very hard. It will take finding a guru or an expert, and they are very, very scarce. It's just not likely to happen any time soon."

This isn't objectively true on a cosmic level; it's a function of the resistance you're engaged with. It's like being in a relationship with an abusive partner. They may say that they're the only person who will ever love you and you couldn't make it on your own. That's not the objective truth, though. That's part of the abuse.

3D energy isn't an abuser, of course--it's here to help us--but it gives us the same skewed perspective that an abuser would. 3D energy insists you can't just let low-vibrational energy go, or that if you can, it must take a very long time and a lot of hard work to do so.

How do you escape this perspective? If you're stuck in 3D energy, you're likely to have thoughts about how hard it is for anything to change, feelings of discouragement, memories of past failures popping into mind, and so on. That's a lot to ignore if you're wanting to make a new energetic choice.

Luckily, you don't really have to fight your thoughts, cheer up, or make yourself believe that things will get easier. Selecting the energy of what you want can happen even when you're crabby, discouraged, and think it's unlikely to work. That's because energy--not thoughts, not emotions--is the real cause of what happens. You just have to keep choosing the energy of what you want, even while your crummy emotions or snippy thoughts are doing their thing. So long as you don't commit energy to those thoughts and emotions, it doesn't matter a whole lot what they are doing. They are just aftereffects of 3D or

4D energy you chose in the past.

The key question to making your life better is: "Can things get easier?" Each level of energy has an answer that tends to pop up in your head when you're at that energy level in that area of your life, whether it be your love life, your finances, your career, or anything else.

Lower 3D energy usually answers the question "Can things get easier?" with "No way! Not gonna happen. It will be this hard--or worse--forever."

Upper 3D promises, "Yes, it will get a little easier...after decades of hard work. Once your kids are raised, or you've retired..."

Lower 4D might say, "It will get easier, but it will take several years of 'doing the inner work.' Get ready for a load of psychotherapy and yoga."

Upper 4D takes the more cheerful approach of expecting months of practicing some technique to make things easier.

At 5D, the answer is, "Of course it can get easier. But I don't care if it gets easier or not, because I'm having so much fun the way it is!"

How easy is it to tell resistant energy you're ready for your manifestation, and it doesn't need to hold you back any longer? The answer that springs to mind has more to do with what energy you're engaging with rather than some objective truth. On a cosmic level, it's just a choice. It's practically instantaneous. You see the resistant energy for what it is--a neutral pattern designed to hold you back for cosmic entertainment purposes-- and you watch it dissolve. Then you touch the energy of what you desire, and it starts to come toward you.

You don't have to believe that things will get easier. Just touch the energy of the repaired house, the new car, the desired manifestation. You don't have to feel the joy of it or believe that you're likely to get it. Just touch the energy of it.

We'll get to how to do this more specifically in the next few sections. The point is, you can shift energy even when your beliefs and emotions aren't very supportive.

As you get in touch with higher energy, your beliefs will shift to become more hopeful and your feelings will lift. Those experiences are effects of the new energy. It's nice when you have hopeful beliefs and happy emotions, but they aren't necessary for beginning the process. They are signposts along the way that spring up naturally, showing you what general energy you've been choosing lately.

SECTION 2: SENSING ENERGY

WHY ENERGY IS SO HARD TO SENSE

Now that we've looked at each of the levels of consciousness, hopefully you have an idea of where your energy may be at in certain areas of your life. If you're like most people, your energy may be in a very stressful, 3D place in one area of your life, and yet be very high-vibrational 5D in a different part of your life. To make our lives easier and more fun, and to manifest our dreams, we shift the 3D or 4D energy in our lives up to 5D.

As I said in the previous chapter, some shifts happen naturally--but what if we want to go faster? In order to shift our vibrations higher more effectively, it helps to be able to sense energy. That's what this group of chapters is all about.

You might wonder why sensing energy seems so foreign. If everything is energy, and energy is so vital to manifesting what we want, then why is it so hard for human beings to sense energy? There are three main reasons why it's hard: 3D's slowness (time), the veil of ignorance, and a lack of vocabulary.

The first reason it's hard for us to sense energy is because 3D experiences separate energetic intentions from their results using time. On the Other Side, your intentions instantly create results. That means it's extremely easy to figure out what kind of energy you are holding at any moment--just look at what's in your face! What is on the outside is an instant reflection of the energy within.

On Earth, however, we have lots of 3D energy that slows

down the manifestation of intentions. Even 4D and 5D energy is slow compared to what we experience on the Other Side. We might intend something quite clearly...and not see it in the outside world for weeks. In the meantime, we've intended a lot of other things. How do we know which specific intention created the fender-bender on the weekend? We don't even like fender-benders! What did we intend, energetically, that was on par with that?

Not only do we not keep track of every energetic intention we have over time, but also, when our intentions are delayed in manifesting, others have more opportunity to interfere (for better or for worse) with our manifestations.

More time means more time for others' intentions to have a say in the outcome. Maybe the person driving the other car had some crummy intentions, and you just happened to be the one cruising by when his fender-bender intention manifested. Or maybe your own energy was barrelling towards a five-car-pile-up, and his energy helped you soften that into a mere bump. Who knows? Again, there's a level of mystification in figuring out how our energy is creating results alongside *other* people's energy creating results.

The second reason it's hard for us to sense energy is because our ability to sense energy directly was deliberately obscured and mystified by souls preparing for the Earth experience.

The ability to sense energy is *pivotal* in figuring out how the universe works. That means if you want to keep a lot of surprise and mystery in life, you need that ability to be dampened.

That's exactly what our souls did in choosing to come to Planet Earth. We deliberately made it hard for ourselves to sense energy, so that we could have long explorations of negativity and drawn-out stories of wanting to getting. Now that most of us are finishing up exploring negativity and long waits, we're ready to re-access our ability to sense energy clearly.

The third reason understanding and sensing energy is

hard is that our vocabulary for energy sensations overlaps with our words for emotions and body sensations. This makes it confusing to tell them apart. Because energy is so subtle, and for so long most people didn't sense it directly, **we don't have much of a vocabulary for energy**.

Consider the vocabulary of wine tasting, which had a similar problem. Wine tasters wind up describing wine flavors as "woody" or "dry" even though there are no wood chips floating around in the goblets and the wine is obviously wet.

We don't have a lot of words for tastes and scents, so wine tasters had to make up words. But if they *completely* made up words, like "frabjakaspooly" and "quabbibla," it would be extremely hard to explain which word meant which exact taste in the wine. There would be no reference point.

Instead, they chose words that *sort of* hinted at a similar sensation in another field. It wasn't the exact same sensation, but there was something similar. Wine is not actually dry, but there's a tiny part that's similar in both "dryness" and certain wines. Wine doesn't have wood chips, but there's something about how wood smells that is sort of like the taste in the wine. It's not ideal language, but they try and pick words that sort of feel like how the wine tastes, and then they learn to use those words in special ways.

Similarly, we don't have words that exactly describe energy (yet!), and energy workers wind up borrowing words to try and express what they're sensing. For better or worse, though, they often pick words that we also use for emotions or body sensations, which winds up confusing things.

An energy worker might describe a particular energy as "high," but we also use "high" to describe certain emotional states like bliss or excitement. Or they might just say a particular energy "feels good," which again overlaps with how we describe emotional states, plus body states.

If an expert in energy says, "Cultivate a high energy that feels good," the ordinary person is likely to think, "Okay, that means I need to make myself feel happy instead of sad." But energy is different from emotion.

Because there's no clear, distinct categories for energy, you have to learn which words best represent energetic states for you personally. The words that work for you may not work for others, and vice versa. It can be easy to get turned off by a particular book or modality simply because they use words that don't jive well with your experience.

You can come up with your own vocabulary for the energy you sense, or you can borrow words that seem close enough to be helpful. Here are some examples of words used for energy:

- Free (versus "constrained, tight")
- Swift (versus "slow-moving, sluggish")
- Open (versus "closed, congested, clogged")
- Light (versus "dark, muddy" or versus "heavy, dense")
- Clear (versus "clouded, confused" or versus "crackly, garbled")
- Spacious (versus "tight, congested, bottled up, trapped")
- Smooth (versus "bumpy, rough" or versus "uneven, wavery, warbling")
- Resonant (versus "discordant, noisy")
- Echo-ey (versus "flat, thin, shallow")
- Solid (versus "flimsy, shallow, withered")
- Electric, tingly, "live wire" (versus "flat, dead wire")

All of these words could be mistaken for body sensations or emotions. I'll go over the difference between sensing energy versus sensing body stuff and emotions in the next few chapters.

As a Law of Attraction (LOA) maverick, you've got to question the words used by experts and see if they match how you experience things. Try out the words from the list above and see if any resonate with you. "When my energy is in a good state, it feels light, open, and spacious" or "When my energy's good, I feel free" or "Good energy to me feels like resonance, thrumming." Or something else--you get the idea. Which words best capture what you sense?

HOW EMOTIONS AND ENERGY SENSATIONS ARE DIFFERENT

Emotions are different from energy sensations. Energy is fundamental and creates everything else, while emotion is an effect. Some LOA books say emotion creates, but they are skipping the energy step.

Energy creates a multitude of effects. Body sensations and emotions are effects that happen very quickly, so they're usually good indicators of what kind of energy you're running. Outer circumstances are effects that take longer to show up, so they can still indicate what you're doing with energy, but not as clearly.

When you keep holding the same energy, the effects compound and get more intense. The emotion gets stronger. The body sensations increase. The outer circumstances pile up. All these are effects of the energy you're holding.

Most of the time how you're feeling is a clue to how you've been vibrating lately. When your energy is at a high level, you tend to have happy, comfy, lighthearted feelings. When your energy is at a low vibration, you tend to have cross, disagreeable, unpleasant feelings. "Tend to have" is a key phrase. It's not a hard-and-fast rule, but it's a general thing that happens. You can't shift energy by shifting emotion very well, but your emotions often tell you something about how you're moving energy. If you feel lousy, *probably* you've been choosing an energy that's not aligned with who you are or what you want.

Emotion can be a helpful indicator of how you've been running your energy, but it's not foolproof. Since there's a delay in time, sometimes great emotions happen while you've got lousy energy, and sometimes lousy emotions happen when you've got great energy. They are two different things.

Although emotion doesn't create anything directly, sometimes you wind up shifting your energy when you manipulate your emotions. This sometimes works, which is why so many LOA books tell you to just rev up your joy, your gratitude, your peace, or whatever other good feeling you can dream up in order to change your life.

When this works, it only works because you've managed to shift the energy underneath. It's not actually the emotion doing anything; it's the energy.

It's like trying to move a cake by moving the frosting alone. If it's a tiny cupcake with a huge cap of stiff frosting, you may be able to move the cupcake from one plate to another just by messing with the frosting. But for anything big, pushing around the frosting does nothing. You're not shifting a six-layer wedding cake by grabbing the buttercream rose. And you're usually not shifting your energy by pushing yourself into an emotion. The energy is so much bigger and stronger. The emotion is a bit of fluffy buttercream by comparison.

Still, the LOA books that emphasize emotion can be helpful at times. For one thing, they help people learn to identify and care about how they're feeling. Frankly, human beings in general have often been pretty clueless about recognizing, labeling, and evaluating what they feel. We think we're just embarrassed about how our presentation at work went, and don't realize there's anger underneath. Or we shout and throw things at a partner, not realizing there's sadness along with the anger.

There is a lot of cultural pressure to deny certain emotions, and often families have unspoken rules about which emotions are "safe" and which they're not allowed to have. This means there are a lot of people out there who just don't know very much about what they're feeling.

For them, being told that their emotions create their circumstances can be helpful, because it makes them pay attention to things they didn't sense before. They start learning more about how they're feeling. They become able to identify very subtle feelings. They are able to tell when more than one emotion is mixed in.

Since energy is even subtler than emotion, telling people "energy attracts" when they can't yet even detect their emotions is sort of pointless. Figuring out exactly what you're feeling is a good first step.

Similarly, the advice to "sit with your feelings" is often helpful as a first step. It gives you a chance to process signals you may be getting about what you're creating. Emotions are part of 3D, 4D, and 5D patterns, and when we stop to really feel them, we notice more about what that pattern is and whether we want to continue it. It can help make you ready to release a really gunky 3D pattern, if you feel all the agitation and anger you have coming from it. If you refuse to feel those feelings, you might cycle through the 3D pattern again and again without understanding how it's harming your life. Fully experiencing the emotions associated with a 3D pattern can make us feel "complete" with it. "Okay, I don't need to do that anymore. I've had the full experience."

That said, sitting with your feelings won't fix everything. Sometimes you can sit with the wrong feeling. I sat with sadness for many years and it didn't budge. It took a book that suggested depression might be repressed anger to make me realize I was sitting with the wrong feeling.

Similarly, I found that sitting with my fear helped it get triggered less and less--but only up to a point. Then it seemed to stop working, and no matter how much time I spent sitting with my fear, I got triggered the same number of times. I now know that an energetic shift is what is really needed, and that's sometimes accomplished by sitting with a feeling, but sometimes not. Again, it's the energy, people!

As my guides said:

You human beings say you must feel all your feelings, and that is a helpful idea for a stage of growth, but as you get closer to Ascension you do not need to feel every emotion in a conscious and visceral way, just as you do not need to feel every toxin you release from your body. Your body can manage escorting toxins out without your conscious witnessing. So it is with emotion.

In other words, processing and releasing emotions is like processing and releasing toxins. If there's something you need to change in the here-and-now, it helps to figure out where the toxin or unpleasant emotion is coming from. If you have lead poisoning because there's lead in your pipes, you need to know about the pipes so you can get that fixed. If your coworker's racism is causing your anger, you need to know that so you can speak up and make your workplace respectful.

Other times, knowing where the toxin or emotion came from isn't that important. If it's from the distant past, your body and your conscious mind don't need to know where it came from. Your body doesn't care if the lead came from the antique toy you had when you were five or the paint in the shed when you were ten. It just detoxes it when it has the resources.

Your emotional processor doesn't care if the anger came from that time your dad said you were dumb or that time a mean kid pushed you down. It just processes it when it has the resources. If there's nothing in your present environment that needs changing, then you don't need to figure out the why and wherefore of your emotions. You can sit with them if that helps, but it's shifting the energy underneath that is the real solution.

Feeling your feelings is often a helpful step to take. Still, the fact remains that emotions aren't everything. Let's look at some examples of how emotions and energy can come apart.

"Good" Emotions, Lousy Energy

It's possible to feel emotions we like, such as happiness, joy, confidence, or power, while having a lousy energetic state.

Although usually a lousy energetic state winds up sending unpleasant emotional signals, this doesn't always line up. I'll give three big examples: bullying yourself into a positive emotion, psychiatric drug effects, and social-expectation-created happiness.

Many of us have had the experience of trying to bully ourselves into a happy feeling in order to manifest good things. It's not just that it's hard--which it often is--it's that even when you get into a so-called "happy" state, something about it feels off.

The sort of bullying pressure behind it *(sadness will make your life even worse, better push into happiness, stay there, stay there, don't let up, push those sad feelings away if they try to come back)* makes any happiness you might achieve feel...strangely unsatisfying and full of effort. If you try to force yourself into an emotion you think will attract a great new job, but your energy is actually aligned with a lousy job, then the happy shiny feeling you push yourself into will feel strained and hollow. When your energy is aligned well, then happy shiny feelings occur without a great deal of effort and will feel full and rich rather than hollow.

Here's the second way in which emotion and energy come apart. People who have taken psychiatric medications sometimes report that they feel more happiness but that the happiness feels strangely aversive and "fake." When this occurs, this is the result of someone trying to force a shift in emotion rather than shifting the energy underneath that generates that emotion. If you've ever had the experience of having an emotion that felt "fake"--I don't mean pretending to someone else that you felt something you didn't, but actually *having* an emotion that felt strangely fake--then you have had a hint that emotion isn't the whole shebang for manifestation.

Social expectations create another kind of mismatch. You can feel happy, but also strangely congested, tight, and sluggish underneath if the happiness is forced by your will or the expectations of society or family.

Getting married to a person you only sort of love? You might feel happy just because you and everyone else have expected for so long that *wedding days are happy days*. But the happiness may be combined with a resistant, sluggish feeling underneath.

Society doesn't recognize how energy plays a role, so it might not understand how anything could be wrong if you're feeling good. *"You got divorced? But you were so happy together..."* If you're new to energy work, you might not understand it either, and misjudge events and situations because you had some happy feelings in them. *"How could it have been wrong if I felt happy? Happiness creates more happiness, right?"* Nope, it's the energy underneath that matters.

Some actions may make you feel better emotionally even while keeping your energy stuck. It might make you feel better, emotionally, to yell at your partner, eat buckets of ice cream when you're sad, or post a mean comment online to increase your own confidence. The question is whether these behaviors are in tune with an energy that helps you manifest what you want, or if their energy is a dense, 3D energy.

Sometimes yelling at your partner really does shift your energy in a good way and is an important part of growth (yelling at an abuser, for example, might help you solidify the self-trust you need to resolve to leave). But often we have go-to emotional boosts that are very 3D and keep us stuck in 3D patterns. Learning to sense the grungy 3D energy underneath the positive feeling can help you ditch any behaviors that are part of a dense, unhelpful pattern.

There are many other cases where people experience positive emotion while running lousy energy patterns, such as great sex with a person you hate, certain kinds of illicit drug use, or taking glee in the suffering of others. You can probably think of your own examples of times you or others have felt good on an emotional level but were actually in a destructive state energetically.

"Bad" Emotions, Better Energy

The opposite can also happen--you can feel terrible while actually improving your energy flow. Again, this doesn't usually happen. Usually our emotions reflect what we're doing with our energy pretty quickly. But there are times when our energy is doing one thing while our emotions are doing something else.

We can illustrate this with an imaginary case. Suppose a woman has a deep trauma she's kept hidden for years (I'll call her Castalia, because it's an awesome name). She's been too scared and ashamed to talk about it to anyone, so Castalia has practiced not thinking about it, and just tries to forget about the whole thing. One day she finally reveals the trauma to a therapist. She describes what happened, and as she does, the pain of the original event comes back and she cries, feeling a lot of sadness and anger.

Now in the usual Law of Attraction sort of schema, what is happening here? Castalia went from feeling relatively normal and neutral to feeling sad and angry. It looks like she's ruining her chances for good things to come into her life, doesn't it?

But intuitively, we can guess that actually this moment of catharsis is good for Castalia. And Castalia can probably sense that, too--even as she's feeling sad and hurt about what happened, she may notice a freedom running underneath that. She may sense a feeling of openness and relaxation even as she's sobbing, a subtle feeling underneath the pain that feels like a release.

This is because although her emotions have gone "down," her energy has actually sprung up to a higher level, one involving truth and honoring herself. What has been pent up and stifled in her energy is now free and clear.

You may have felt this dichotomy of experience yourself: a moment when you had "negative" emotion, and yet felt freer and lighter in energy at the same time.

Here's another example. Suppose there's a longstanding racial discrimination happening, and you finally get angry enough to stand up and address it. You might feel emotionally very angry and yet energetically spacious, full of energetic empowerment for the good of all. That's angry emotion and spacious energy together. That isn't a low-vibrational state, even though traditional LOA says anger is bad. You can feel negative emotion and still feel free, swift, open, light, clear, and spacious in certain circumstances. It doesn't usually happen, which is why we call them *negative* emotions in the first place, but it does happen sometimes.

Energy is Fundamental

Now, as I've argued, emotion is not the same thing as energy, and striving for an emotional state doesn't always work well because emotions are the effect of energy, not the cause. You're better off focusing on the energetic state of your manifestation. Trying to do this work on the emotional level is better than nothing, but it's not going to be as effective as doing it on the energetic level.

Identifying what your desired manifestation is like energetically is harder to put into words because we just don't have a lot of language yet to describe these kinds of states. Luckily, you have an innate intuitive grasp on these things from your eons spent on the Other Side, where you instantly attuned to any energy you chose and got instant feedback.

Here, the feedback is slower, making us get confused about energy more often, but we can still have an intuitive grasp on how to attune to the energy we want. As a maverick, you'll have your own unique way of doing this, but there will be some advice when we get to our 5D toolbox. But for now, let's continue to examine how to sense energy.

HOW BODY SENSATIONS AND ENERGY SENSATIONS ARE DIFFERENT

Your body can give you lots of clues about how you've been running energy lately. When you meet someone new, your body may signal you as to whether their energy is uplifting or dragging. Many people discover that paying attention to physical sensations helps them discern what is helpful or unhelpful in their lives.

If you find you get a lot of insight from listening to your body, then by all means continue that practice. The point where things go wrong is in assuming that your body *always* gives you correct signals about energy.

Energetic sensations are different from body sensations. If you're an especially kinesthetic person, you may translate a lot of your energy-sensing into body sensations, but they are fundamentally different. Your body sensations may give you good clues about energy in a general way, but it's important to be aware that it's not a foolproof method.

There are four reasons why body sensations differ from energy: a difference in where the sensing occurs, a mismatch in terms, high vibrations occurring with bad body sensations, and low vibrations occurring with good body sensations.

Energy Sensations Often Occur Outside the Body

Many times when people sense energy, they sense it as being outside their body. This may be as simple as an aura that stretches beyond your body's skin, or as mysterious as sensing a low-vibrational field twenty feet ahead and to the left. There are no bodily nerves involved in such sensing. Energy may often register for your bodily nerves, but it is still something different from them. It is deeper and more fundamental than anything your tissues, nerves, or skin could feel at the physical level.

Even if you are outside your body completely, flying in the astral realms, (or dead!), you can still sense energy. It's a function of your soul, fundamentally. If thinking of energy sensations as being similar to body sensations helps you, use that. Just be aware that not all of your body's cues will align with energy.

Kinesthetic Terms Often Don't Match the Energy Sensation

Even when people use kinesthetic words for describing energy, they usually don't mean them the way we mean them in a body context. For example, feeling "expanded" in an energetic sense doesn't necessarily mean that you feel like your spine has lengthened or your tummy has gotten bigger. Feeling energetically "congested" doesn't mean your lungs feel full of mucus. In these cases, expansion and congestion are not body sensations. They are energetic sensations. Like calling a wine "dry," they are just metaphors. They capture a feeling similar to the body sensation but not exactly like it.

High Vibrations, Terrible Body Sensations

We can also see the difference between body sensations and energy sensations by showing examples of cases where they come apart. Usually our body's state reflects what our energy has been lately. But this isn't always the case. Sometimes very unpleasant body sensations accompany very high energy.

For example, a very evolved person might nevertheless have a terminal illness. They might experience many body sensations of pain, weariness, and sluggishness while still having very high vibrations. Similarly, a person addicted to a drug might experience intense withdrawal symptoms as they wean themselves off of it. Their energy may be becoming expanded and higher, while their body is screaming with every nerve.

Imagine a rock climber who absolutely loves climbing a sheer cliff face. Her muscles may be very tense and constricted while she clings to the rock, but her energy may be quite relaxed, open, and flowing for all that. She may feel physically tired while energetically re-energized. Her body is tense, constricted, and weary, but her energy is relaxed, open, and energized.

Subconscious prejudice can send you bad body signals as well. Media repeatedly portrays young black men as "dangerous." Suppose you are in the hospital and you discover your body tenses up at the times when a young black doctor enters the room to treat you and relaxes at the times when a white male doctor treats you. That doesn't mean that the black doctor must have had low vibes and the white doctor must have had good vibes. Instead, it may be your body reflecting years of subconscious programming saying that young black men are unsafe while doctors who are white males are "proper" authorities.

The body can send unhelpful and untruthful signals when prejudice is involved. Some body sensations are not signalling energetic truth, but are instead reflecting bad programming from society.

Subconscious prejudice will express in body sensations, but prejudice is not high vibrational, and the body's cues under prejudice may not show you anything about high-vibrational energy.

Low Vibrations, Pleasing Body Sensations

Just as sex with a person you hate or certain kinds of drug use can cause some gleeful emotion, they can also cause fantastic body sensations, even while the energy underneath might be lousy. Having enjoyable body sensations doesn't always mean the energy you've got going on is good.

The most common mistake LOA practitioners make with this is assuming that a relaxed body means you are in a good energetic state. A relaxed body just means your body is not sending very many signals at the moment. You can have a very relaxed body while still having dreadful energy.

For example, if you're asleep having a nightmare, your body is still pretty dang relaxed! There may be a little bit of tension while you're dreaming something distressing, but it's still nowhere near the tension in your body during your delightful dance class or running for the bus.

Telling the Difference between Energy and Irrelevant Body Sensations

If you're a very kinesthetic person, kinesthetic-sounding words may appeal to you when you're describing energy. That's okay. Just keep in mind that the real congestion, sluggishness, or tension you're sensing energy-wise is not the same thing as clogged lungs, tired muscles, or tense muscles, and that you may sense energy very far from *any* part of your body!

The best way to distinguish the two is just to practice. Try treating the sensation as if it were energy, and see if it works out. Try treating it as if it were just a body glitch, and see if that works out.

If you feel a tightening sensation when you think about trying that new Italian restaurant, is that energy talking or just nerves or a bit of mold in your throat? If it's not too dangerous, just try out the restaurant and see what happens. Trial and error is slow but really does work.

If you'd like a little more intellectual guidance, here's my take. In general, energetic sensations will feel subtler, "deeper," and less triggering than body sensations. Overwhelmingly bad energy signals almost never happen. They're saved for life-and-death scenarios. In general, bad energy feels like a subtler "not for me" or vaguely icky feeling. It also feels deeper, in the sense that you're sensing something more than just how something seems in appearance, logic, or past experience.

In the end, if you feel drawn to exploring energy through body sensations, you'll have to be a maverick and find your own vocabulary, principles, and methods. What works for others may not work for your body. So long as you remember the body does not always reflect your current energy, you'll find your own way of figuring out what works.

HOW THE CONTENT OF YOUR THOUGHTS IS DIFFERENT FROM ENERGY MANIPULATION

A common adage in LOA books is "thoughts become things." Is this true?

What really creates is energy. When we intend on an energetic level, sometimes thoughts accompany that. As you're intending a deep, 5D energy, feelings of love and thoughts like "I bless everyone" or "Love is all" may come up. As you're deeply intending a new car, feelings of freedom and thoughts like "I want a new car" or "New cars are great!" might come up. These feelings and thoughts are not doing the creating. They are effects, not causes. The real cause is the energy underneath.

This means there is both good news and bad news.

The good news is that policing your thoughts is not necessary. If you randomly start thinking about something bad, there's no reason to freak out. If you get frustrated and think, "My manifestation is never going to happen," you are not shooting yourself in the foot. Your energy may still be deeply aligned, even if a few stray thoughts of negativity come up.

The bad news is simply repeating thoughts, like in

affirmations or verbal intentions, may not do anything, either. If you're repeating, "I have a new car" over and over, but your energy is still firmly 3D about cars, you're not likely to get a new one. And even if you did, the car would be a match to that 3D energy, which means it would wind up not being not much better than your current situation. Maybe the new car would break down a lot, or be too cramped, or come with a massive monthly payment.

Trying to create with your thoughts doesn't work very well for most people, because most of the time, changing our thoughts doesn't shift our energy. If affirmations *do* work for you, it's because you wind up tapping into a different energetic state. It's not the words or the thoughts per se; it's the energy underneath that winds up making the difference.

You've probably already noticed two kinds of problems for the "thoughts become things" idea: stuff that shows up without our thinking about it, and stuff that doesn't show up however much we think about it.

Most of the background of your life includes things you have spent little, if any, time thinking about. You may not think a lot about board games, new Kpop songs, and hockey scores, and yet they keep happening in the periphery of your life.

You may not think much about air pressure that is the right state for human beings, atmospheric protection from cosmic rays, and cellular mitosis, and yet these things are happening nonstop in your life and are vital to your survival.

Thinking a lot of thoughts about cellular mitosis (or even the lack of it) is not going to do much to your body one way or the other. Most people's subconscious minds are not thinking about these things, either--heck, kids don't even know what cellular mitosis and cosmic rays are. It's not your conscious mind nor your subconscious mind creating these. You get a lot of the circumstances of your life for "free", no thinking required.

Some stuff, of course, never shows up even though we think a lot about it. Millions of mothers worry that their kids will be hit by cars or kidnapped, and yet few (compared to the millions) actually do. That repetitive, daily worrying doesn't manifest in kids getting mowed down left and right.

Perhaps you have repetitive fears and worries about becoming homeless, being in a plane crash, or some other event, and yet that event not only is *not* a regular thing in your life-- it may have *never* happened to you, even after years of thinking about it!

This can't be explained by saying you're focusing on the "lack" of something. That's the typical response LOA authors have for the money-hungry user of the Law of Attraction: "You think you're thinking about money all day long, and you're wondering why you're not a millionaire. But you're really thinking about the *lack* of money, and that's what you're creating: the *lack* of money." But the worried mother is not thinking about the lack of kidnappers, and the phobic airline passenger is not thinking about the lack of plane crashes. They really are thinking about something over and over and not getting it.

The contents of your mind are usually your mind just guessing what is going on with life. Because our minds are biologically tilted towards noticing negativity, expecting sameness, and prioritizing whatever is physical, our minds don't pay a lot of attention to energy at first. But energy is the real cause of everything! That means our minds are always trying to play catch-up with the world. Our minds are always scouring the physical world, trying to figure out what causes what, while the *real* causes are energetic intentions the mind doesn't notice.

The contents of our minds rattle around and do very little in the world. It matters less what particular thoughts you have and more what energy you are engaged with.

If framing particular thoughts is a modality you use *for shifting energy*, then that can work well. But the focus should be on whether you are noticing and achieving that energy shift, rather than how many times you repeated a sentence or whether the word "wealth" or "riches" is the right one to use.

Pay attention to the energy, and you'll learn which words,

if any, help you get into the right state. Pay attention to the energy, and you'll know when you need a little more time getting into the energy of sweet romance and when another dozen repetitions of "I have a sexy-hot honey" isn't going to do anything for you.

What about Fear-Based Thoughts?

More modern LOA authors are dumping old terms and using newer, more specific ones. "Fear-based" thoughts is a concept that goes a little deeper than "thoughts become things." Instead, it's more like "thoughts coming from a perspective of fear cause bad things, thoughts coming from a perspective of love cause good things."

This is an improvement because a *perspective* is more general and more encompassing than a particular thought, so it's closer to what really creates, which is energy.

It also acknowledges that the same thought may register differently depending on what perspective you have. According to this view, "There's only three days left before Christmas!" may be a positive-creating thought if you're a kid eager for presents, while the exact same thought may be fear-based for the kid's uncle, who only just started his Christmas shopping.

"Fear-based" is usually contrasted with "heart-centered" (in other words, love-based). Anytime emotion words start getting used, I tend to become cautious, because it's not emotion that creates. It's not the emotion of fear that's really the problem, it's the energetic state we *usually* associate with fear. It's the grabby, pushy energy underneath fear that is the real problem and the real creator.

Likewise, it's not the affective feeling of love that creates higher vibrational things, but rather the expanded, open, gentle-yet-powerful energetic state we associate with that feeling.

This means you still don't have to police your thoughts to see if they have a fearfully-based perspective. Taking time to consider an economic downturn and what your company can do to weather it if it happens may seem like a fear-based thought. Being scared that your company might go under can be a good thing or a bad thing, depending on the energy underneath. If your energy is tangled, harsh, or (pick your negative energy word of choice), then that moment of fear is keeping you stuck in 3D energy and pulling more 3D experiences to you. If your energy is open, clear, or (pick your positive energy word of choice), then that moment of fear is not harmful. It's helping you prepare and draw in higher vibrational things.

Instead of asking, "Is this thought based in love or fear?", try asking "How does my energy feel right now?" The thought might be opening up your energy. It might be closing it down. It might be having no effect. (Like most thoughts!)

So What Are We Supposed to Think?

You don't actually have to think anything. You can create with energy using nonverbal intentions instead of verbalized thoughts. All of us had nonverbal intentions for years before we learned a language, and conscious entities that don't have any language are still using nonverbal intentions exclusively. You can intend without words, with pure energy.

That sounds super-complicated and mystical, but really it's the same basic function you use all the time with indexicals (words like "this" and "that"). Suppose you go on a walk with your best friend, and you see a cat climbing a tree off to the left, two kids playing tag off to the right, and a bird overhead bopping from branch to branch like it's disco time. You say, "That's so cute!", meaning the cat. You could have meant the kids, but you didn't. You could have meant the bird, but you didn't. The word "that" could have intended a multitude of things, but you really only intended one: the cat climbing the tree. That's the kind of intentionality you can have with energy. It's something internal deciding, rather than just letting context or the dictionary-meaning of words determine intention.

Your friend might say, "But how did you *know* that you saying 'That's so cute!' was about the cat? Those exact same words could have pointed out the bird or the kids." And you'd have to say, "I know because I *meant* it that way. That was what

I was *trying* to say." In other words, your intention in saying it made the difference.

It's intention and energy that matters. You can form intentions and manipulate energy by using verbal thoughts if you want to, but you don't have to. The point is to shift energy. If thinking particular thoughts helps you do that, then by all means, do that. Just remember that the real point of attraction is energy. Most techniques in other books you've read about talk about changing thoughts or feelings, but when they work (if they work) it's because you wind up shifting the energy *beneath* your thoughts and emotions.

Energy is very subtle, and lots of human beings don't sense it directly very well. So telling people to change the way they are thinking or feeling is not terrible advice--it's the best that can be done, for many. As Earth develops spiritually, sensing energy directly will become easier and easier, and more and more people will ditch the advice about nitpicking whether a thought is phrased in a "positive" or "negative" way and just go with how the energy feels.

HOW TO MAKE AN ENERGETIC CHOICE

So now we've looked at how to sense energy--how to tell it apart from your emotions, your body sensations, and your thoughts. But we don't just want to sense the energy we have; we want to be able to change it at will. For manifesting, we want to change stuck, jangly, dissonant energy to smooth, flowing, resonant energy. So how do we do that?

How do you actually make an energetic choice? I don't mean *which* energy should you choose, but once you know the energy you want, *how* do you actually select it?

If you're unfamiliar with the idea of an energetic choice, you may be looking for a "Step 1, Step 2, Step 3" sort of thing. But selecting an energy is your most basic free will choice. Nothing so basic and fundamental to the universe has a "Step 1, Step 2" sort of structure.

Your choice of energy exists not only in the Earthly 3D timeline, but also in nonlinear existence. Even when you don't have a body and do not exist in linear time, you still have the choice of which energy to experience. Without linear time, there's nothing you do first, second, third. It all happens at once.

It's possible that there's something even more fundamental in the universe than energy, but my guides say that in Earthly terms, energy is as deep as we get:

Your free will choice, applied to energy, is everything. Awakening is about becoming consciously aware of your energetic choices and how those choices play out in physical reality.

Asking, "How do I make an energetic choice?" is like

asking, "How do I lift my arm?" when you're not tied up or paralyzed. There's no explanation. You just do it. The moment you intend it, it starts happening. You just decide to lift your arm, and your arm goes up. Choosing an energy happens in a similar way. You just decide which energy you want, and that's that.

Sanaya Roman in her channelling has something similar to say about holding and radiating light:

"Your intuitive understanding of what light is and how to connect with it is more important than any definitions I could give you. The more light your body can hold, the higher your vibration and the greater your ability to transform the energy around you into a higher order."

She doesn't try to explain exactly what light is, and she doesn't give a step-by-step full analysis of how to go about connecting with the light. At some point, you have to rely on intuition. (Such a drag if you've always relied on your intellect! But alas, it seems inescapable. If you find a good way to explain how to attune energy directly in words, please share it with the world! We could use some mavericks working on this.)

The Bad News about Making Energetic Choices

There are two caveats to choosing energy, though. One is that you have to know at least somewhat which energy you want. If you're too vague, you might not land on the energy you thought you wanted. That's like intending, "I want to move some limb or other, not sure which one...An arm, maybe? Or a leg? Something..." If the intention is too unclear, you might not move any of them, or you might move all of them, or you might move your neck instead just because you don't know what's what!

The other caveat is that your intention has to be truly meant. Often in self-help circles, people describe intentions as sentences in your head. They do this so often that people think all they need to do to "set an intention" is think a particular sentence in their minds. "I intend to have a lot of money." Repeating a statement isn't necessarily intending. You could repeat "I intend to have a lot of money" over and over without *really* meaning it as "I'm *doing* this. I'm not just saying it."

Usually, when people claim they are setting intentions, what they are really doing is forming a wish and repeating it to themselves. Trying to intend outer things like money doesn't work that well because in linear time, the arrival of the money comes much later. It's hard to feel like *I'm doing this now* when you know it may be weeks before the cash actually shows up!

Energy, on the other hand, changes instantly when you change intentions. There is no time lag at all in your shift in energy. There will be a time lag in your emotions, body sensations, outer circumstances, and bags of coins falling at your feet, but the energy you're radiating will change instantly. That makes it easier to intend energy than to intend some outward circumstance.

Richard Dotts notes that nonverbal intentions often seem to have more power. In other words, when you can sense the energy you want and intend it without saying words to yourself, your intentions become a lot cleaner and homed-in on what you want. It's just too easy to repeat words without really meaning them. It's easy to fool yourself that you are intending the energy of money (when you're not!) if your mental dialogue says, "I intend lots of money! I intend this energy! Here we go!" or some such thing.

If, instead of telling yourself "I intend the energy that aligns with lots of money," you just know what that sort of energy feels like and intend that energy, you don't get bogged down in words. And you don't waste time repeating words that you don't realize you don't actually mean through-and-through.

I'm not against using words if that helps you focus, but make sure you can really feel yourself selecting an energy. Don't get distracted by the words and think that mental chatter is enough. It's a choice you make on the level of energy, not on the level of words.

The Good News

When you start to overanalyze "How do I make an energetic choice, anyway? How do I use this free will people say I have?" it starts to sound impossibly complicated. The good news is that it's not. It's instinctive, natural, and effortless. You are already doing it a million times a day. You already intuitively know how to do this. It just starts to sound crazy hard when we try to put something that basic and instinctive into words.

It's as if we tried to explain how to lift an arm by saying, "First, contract the muscle in the back of your upper arm, while tensing the outer muscles slightly so your arm doesn't go wildly flapping aside. Oh, and make sure your cells don't run out of energy as they begin this work--give them lots of ATP to burn...." You already intuitively know how to lift your arm, even if you're a little kid. You just do it.

Since you're already making energetic choices every moment of every day, the question is not so much figuring out how to choose, but rather just *noticing* the choices you're already making. Your conscious mind may or may not be very aware of the energetic choices you're making. Many of those choices will be on automatic. They will be choices you make because you sense other people using energy that way, or because it seemed helpful when you were a kid, or for other reasons that may not be relevant anymore. As you become more aware of your energetic choices, you notice what you like and what you don't like.

In other words, when you learn to sense energy, you naturally begin to choose differently. You notice your energy getting gunky and gross after lunch one day, and so you wind up shifting to an energy that feels cleaner and smoother. You notice your energy runs high and light when you're taking a walk in nature, so you recapture that sensation as you're driving downtown, knowing it's still available to you.

It can take practice, of course, to automate your new choices of energy. You might worry, "Well, I've spent decades rehearsing bad energy! How is me remembering to check in with my energy and do something different with it a few times a day ever going to undo that?"

Luckily, it's easier than you think. Though you may have spent years doing things the uncomfortable way, energy-wise, once you realize it's a choice and that a different way feels better, the change happens relatively smoothly.

It's like having a habit of sitting in an uncomfortable chair. Once you realize there are other chairs, and that they feel better to sit in, you're going to sit in those plush, comfy chairs more often. Every once in a while you may forget and sit in the poky, hard chair again out of habit. But the fact that the other chairs *feel* better makes it easier to remember in the moment, and you begin sitting comfortably more and more. And if you do sit in the poky chair, you know you can get out of it right away and swap to something better.

Our natural state is free-flowing, unhampered, high-vibrational energy. It's our default on the Other Side. So shifting energy is more a matter of letting the habits of choosing low vibes we picked up on Earth go ahead and dissolve.

As we continue to stroll around on planet Earth, we tend to pick up more low-vibe energy from mimicking other people, so sometimes we have to go back and clear our energy again and again. But the more skilled you get at noticing how your energy is feeling, the less likely you are to keep picking up unwanted energies and the faster you get at releasing them when you do pick them up.

If you notice that your energy starts to feel stuck and sluggish after watching the evening news, for example, then with practice you get better at handling the situation. You might decide to watch the news less often, or you might notice the sluggishness as soon as it starts happening and release it instead, or you even (at a master level) might simply intend that it no longer affect you.

Now that you know more intellectually about what energy is, let's move on to doing something with it.

EXERCISES FOR PRACTICING SENSING ENERGY

Even if you never practice, you will still eventually develop the ability to sense energy. Part of it will come through trial and error naturally in your life.

Another part will come from being around a master manifestor (whether they are some sort of official LOA teacher, or more likely, just someone in your life who is good at getting what they want with ease). When we are around a master making a deep energetic choice, we remember a little of how to do that ourselves by that inspiration. You can "catch" the skill without having to learn it consciously.

That said, if you'd like to fast-track your ability to directly sense energy, here are some ideas.

The Basic Exercise

If you'd like a brief exercise in smoothing out your energy, here's what to do.

First, let your body and emotions settle down. You can lie down, breathe slowly, journal your worries, sit with your feelings--it really doesn't matter exactly what, so long as you get your body and emotions to settle down enough that they won't distract you. Otherwise, they may make it harder for you to sense your energy underneath all that. This may take only a second or two if you're feeling fine, or hours if you're in crisis!

What about thoughts? Should you try to make your mind empty and clear?

In my experience, it's not worthwhile trying to still your thoughts. Thoughts don't do very much, and they are very difficult for most people to stop entirely. It's better to just let thoughts pop up as they will, and just consider them white noise in the background. Stray thoughts may pop up while you're focusing on your energy, just like stray thoughts might pop up while you're writing an email. They're a momentary distraction but not enough to keep you from doing what you need to do.

Once you feel fairly neutral and fairly undistracted, it's time to sense your current energy. Notice if there's any energy that feels convoluted, constricted, heavy, brassy, stinky-- whatever your metaphor of choice is.

Next, again using whatever wording or metaphor works for you, intend that your energy unsnaggle and get clear. You can focus on "opening up," "getting lighter," "letting negativity drain out," "smoothing out the wrinkles and bumps," or whatever other idea feels intuitively helpful to you. For this to work, you have to remember to *be gentle* (don't force your energy one way or another) and *intend a shift.*

Remember, the resistant energies are actually trying to help you by giving you a long, exciting journey towards your end goal instead of a boring, quick, instant manifestation. They already want to help you, but they need to be signalled what to do.

Don't treat them as an enemy to get rid of or bully. If you get pushy, the resistant energies figure you want a new, long, drawn-out journey of fighting with resistance, and they'll be happy to oblige! That's why it's important to be gentle. "Hey, resistance, let's go ahead and smooth out. No hurry, though. Thanks for holding me back in the past, but I think I'm ready to have what I want now. When you're ready, let 'er rip." Let the energy smooth out without a lot of micromanaging or fussing. All the energy of the universe wants to support you.

Now, since you've probably practiced holding your energy

in a snagged-up way, your energy may go back to the old pattern at some point. This usually only happens if you feel triggered by something.

Here's an example. Let's suppose Rodrigo wants to manifest an awesome boyfriend. He's tried vision boards and that sort of thing, but hasn't had a lot of traction. When he thinks about having a boyfriend, he feels excited, but he also feels a sort of clammy, sluggish energy underneath.

Rodrigo decides to try shifting his energy. He relaxes a bit, puts on some soothing music, and intends that his energy become warm and fluid (his metaphor of choice for energy). He thinks about having a boyfriend and what that would be like, and his energy starts to clog up a bit, but he quickly redirects his energy to be warm and flowing again. After a few minutes, he feels like the shift is going to last, so he goes about his business.

At work he has a good day, but then as he's leaving, a friend invites him to a party. "You should come!" the friend says. "After all, it's not like you have a date or anything. You're not going to be busy."

Rodrigo feels triggered by this comment. He worries that his friend is right and that he is foolish to expect finding a special someone. His psyche, stung by the comment, reverts back to the old energy pattern of clammy sluggishness. Now Rodrigo will probably need another session of readjusting his energy.

Luckily, since he already did it once, his system knows what to aim for and it's a little easier to warm up and flow his energy more smoothly. Later in the week, Rodrigo gets triggered a couple more times, once by seeing a romantic comedy that made him feel envious and longing, and once just by sitting thinking glum thoughts about relationships as he sipped his coffee. He eventually finds a spare moment to readjust his energy, though, and he's back on track.

That's the basic exercise. Let your body and emotions settle down enough that they don't distract you. Then sense the energy around the topic of your manifestation. Then intend that

that energy "smooth out," "tingle," "rev up"--whatever energy state seems best to you. Repeat as needed.

Comparison Exercise

This exercise helps you feel the difference between emotion and energy.

Think of a time in your life when you felt really good-- either really happy, or really powerful and "in the zone." Try not to pick a time where society or family members had strong expectations that it *should* be a happy, good-feeling time. In other words, try not to pick a graduation, the birth of a baby, an engagement, or any other moment where there's a strong "You really SHOULD feel happy, or you're just an ungrateful selfish beast" vibe to it. It's not that those are unhappy moments, it's just that sometimes the expectation of happiness creates a "pushiness" that we don't need influencing the exercise.

Maybe you felt happy paddling on a lake, or waving to your friends from your car. It doesn't have to look like an earth-shattering moment to anyone else, it just has to feel really good to you. Try to remember what it felt like. If it feels natural to you, relive it a little. What words come to mind, if you had to describe it? Then drop the memory.

Next, I want you to get yourself into a super-high, super-happy state, and I want you to PUSH to do it. Force yourself up into happiness. Get happier. Make yourself get happier still. Lift the joy up even higher. Raise yourself higher STILL, higher than you thought you could go. You thought that was it? Push even HIGHER. Now notice how you are feeling--happy, but also some sort of other feeling that probably doesn't feel right. What is that other feeling? What is it like? Where do you notice it in your body? (Again, body sensations are not the be-all and end-all, but they can help.)

So now you have two experiences, one in which your energy was probably in a very good state (your happy memory) and one in which your energy was strained or off (the force-yourself-to-feel-as-happy-as-possible moment).

What exactly was different between the two happinesses? We call both feelings "happy," and yet there is a distinct difference that makes the first one better than the second. It's not even a difference in degree, since you may have forced yourself to a happier level in the second part of the exercise than you felt in your past memory happy moment. In the second part of the exercise, you basically pushed your energy into a wrong state. So what shape did that wrongness take? Did you feel stuck? Tense? Charged-up in a bad way? Bottled up? Sticky? Heavy? Buzzing? How would you describe it with words? If you can't use words, can you still sense a difference between the two, enough where you might recognize it again?

Check in and Guess Exercise

For this method, pick one of the sets of words from the list in "Why Energy is So Hard to Sense" (or some other set of words that makes intuitive sense to you) for good and bad energy states.

As you go about your day, periodically ask yourself, "If I had to pick one or the other, which would I say my energy is right now?" Of course you don't know for sure--that's why you're practicing--but just try to guess. At first, your guesses will probably align with your emotions, "Well, I'm happy that my coworker is back from vacation, so I guess I'm 'spacious.'" But try and feel into yourself and see if you sense any "spaciousness" anyway.

As you keep trying, every once in a while you'll notice that although your feelings are neutral ("It's been a so-so day"), you do feel one way or the other energetically. "I'm not happy or sad, but I do feel kind of congested. I don't mean that my chest is tight or my muscles are tight, I mean something *underneath* all that body stuff."

As you get more skilled, you'll have times where you notice that your emotions are "high" while your energy vibration is "low", or vice versa. Those times are rarer and require more skill to detect, but they do happen.

What if I Still Can't Sense Anything?

If you keep trying to sense energy and just don't seem to feel anything, here's what to do:

Make sure you don't have any unacknowledged emotions that may be distracting or blocking you. If your wisest friend knew everything about your life, would they say you have an emotion you've been resisting and denying? Some unexpressed anger? Sadness your family doesn't have time for? It's hard to feel something as subtle as energy when there's an unacknowledged emotion clouding things.

If there's no emotional distraction or blockage, try a different set of words. It could be the ones you picked sounded helpful at first but just don't jive with how you feel things. If you were debating between some of the sets listed here, try a different pair of them.

If, however, you already picked the one that seemed obviously best for you from this list and it still didn't work out, and you tried the Comparison exercise and it didn't help, then you are being pushed to find your own way of intuiting energy. It will be different from mine, and probably different from other energy workers' as well.

When you have an honest desire to succeed at something, you're sure you want this for your own joy and not to please or impress others, you've tried with good effort what others do, and what they do just doesn't work for you, you are being called to pioneer a new route.

I'm not sure what that will look like for you. It might just mean you choose words not from this list. Or it might mean that you sculpt a totally new way of looking at energy or a new modality. It can be frustrating not being able to take a method from others right off-the-shelf, but it's also satisfying to create something new that works just for you.

Hopefully this has gotten you started on forming your own ideas about what energy is like in your life and how to tell when you are in a good state energetically and when you are in a bad state energetically. Next, we'll address how you make the shift from low vibrations to 5D energy so that your manifestations will flow.

SECTION 3: THE 5D TOOLBOX

INTRODUCTION
TO 5D TOOLS

To manifest what you want, it's key to move from the 3D or 4D energy you currently have around that topic to 5D. This group of chapters is all about how to make that shift.

5D-level tools are tools of intention and energy, and they are immensely powerful. Almost any tool or practice can be done at the 5D level. The difference is in the quality of the energy involved. If you're using high-vibrational, 5D energy, that shifts your outer and inner worlds far more than any outward action or inner thinking and feeling does.

Take visualization as an example. Most people with lots of 3D energy will not even try it, and if they do, they will generally have lousy results, or only permit results that fit with a scientific, neurologically-based outlook (such as visualization for sports).

At the 4D level, people get more results with visualization, but they think it is the mental picturing and emotion that is creating change. They may get very fussy about what exactly they picture (from a first-person perspective? Third-person perspective?) and which exact emotion they use (is gratitude good, or does that involve too much surprise that you got what you wanted?).

If you choose to visualize at 5D (and you may not, because with 5D energy you do things for fun, and visualizing may not feel that fun for you), you know it's about energy, not pictures or emotions. Your visualization is geared to make the most of a particular energy state, and whatever emotions you cultivate or pictures you bring to mind are in the service of that energy.

Which pictures resonate with you may change from day to day, or even minute to minute. The emotion that aligns with that energy may differ from day to day as well. Instead of fussing over the details of the visualization, you simply target the energy, and allow whatever feels fun and conducive to that energy to arise.

The main tools in our 5D toolbox are asking for help from higher-vibrational beings, taking an attitude of energetic openness, releasing judgyness, and not bullying yourself. We'll go into these in detail.

But first, I'd like to acknowledge that picking up any new tool--even powerful 5D ones--sometimes doesn't work out as planned. In the next section, I'd like to go over some ways in which 5D tools can be misapplied or troublesome. This way, you'll know what to watch out for. After that, we'll dive into more detail on the methods for shifting to 5D.

HOW 3D ENERGY CAN SABOTAGE 5D ADVICE

5D tools and advice, as we've said, are all about intention and energy. Most Law of Attraction (LOA) writers have risen to 4D or 5D in their overall vibrations, but most of the areas of life we have trouble with are stuck in 3D energy. When 5D tools and advice are given to those especially stuck in 3D energy, things do not always go as planned.

For example, one piece of advice that is often given by those in 5D is: "Do what you love." There are a number of problems that might emerge if the person accepting the advice is struggling with 3D energy:

- **The advice may seem ridiculously out-of-touch or airy-fairy.** Because 3D energy is full of struggle, often 5D advice seems too easy or trite compared to the thrashing and struggling the person is going through. ("Do what I love? I'm working 60 hours, the price of childcare keeps going up, and I've just been diagnosed with another health problem. When am I supposed to do what I love? This is *so* unrealistic!")

- **3D energy may make the advice seem very, very tricky and strangely complicated.** Again, 3D is the energy of hardship and struggle, so it will dip whatever it receives into a stinky mire of complication. ("What do they mean, do what you *love*? I like a few things. Is that enough? What about breathing? I'm not sure I love breathing. Should I stop if I don't love it?")

- **The advice may be understood and applied from a 3D level, creating 3D results.** In other words, the person thinks they're following the 5D advice, but since 5D is always, always, always about energy, if you're not using good energy, you're following the letter rather than the spirit of the rule. Advice like "Do what you love" is splashed over a multitude of books and podcasts. "Just do what you love, and bliss will follow!" "Choose a job you love, and you'll never have to work a day of your life." "Go with the flow, the feeling of love, and your water bill will get paid somehow." This kind of advice sounds like it is saying, "Take an outward action that makes you feel a particular emotion." In reality, it's about an *energy* underneath emotion and *that energy* inspiring action, but it's easy to gloss over this detail in a pink-font, glittery hardback coffee table book.

Trying to apply the advice with 3D energy produces 3D results. "Do what I love? Well, what I'd love is to have a beer on the job. Hey, I got fired! Your stupid LOA ideas don't work." "I ate only the foods I love, and I gained twenty pounds!" "I fired all the employees I didn't love, and now my company is really struggling." Without the 5D energy, the real advice can't be applied. The real advice isn't about doing things to give yourself an emotional buzz. It's about getting in touch with a certain kind of energy FIRST, which feels good and which then inspires helpful action.

- **The advice may be applied with mixed energy (partly 5D, partly 3D), creating mixed results.** This is very common and is a natural part of the process of shifting vibrations. After all, most of us are not going to succeed with running heart-based, 5D energy about our topic of concern 24/7. Sooner or later, we touch some unpleasant 3D stickiness when we think about that new car or new sweetheart we want to manifest. Old 3D patterns will pop up and taint our results from time to time. We just have to keep practicing working on our energy. If the changes you're making are small, then it's not a big deal when a glitch pops up in your manifesting. If you're making sweeping changes, though, then it can be painful to have a spectacular failure just when you thought you were getting somewhere. For this reason, some LOA writers advise making your energetic changes slowly, rather than spending all weekend meditating on gratitude and sending love notes to everyone. That prevents some spectacular crashes, but it also means you may wait longer for your life to evolve to a 5D vibration, and in the meantime you will have the "normal life" 3D hiccups and annoyances to deal with. It's up to you whether you want to hurry the process or not.

- **The advice may be correctly applied, but because it is at such a different level, it creates so much temporary chaos that people quit.** This is similar to the mixed energy case, but here, nothing (from a soul perspective) *bad* is happening, it just seems bad because it's a big, sudden change that you didn't expect. 5D energy is powerful, and it will tear apart the 3D structures in your life. That might make you feel abandoned if you're not sure what's going on. Of course, if you keep up the 5D energy, eventually new, better, 5D structures will emerge. But it's a big ask for someone to go through that much chaos for months and months while their whole life realigns with substantially higher energy. Most people are uncomfortable with that much shocking change in a short period of time.

For example, suppose you've been running a lot of 5D energy around the topic of career. You realize you'd like a better job, one that really makes your heart sing. "I need to leave this low-vibration job. I guess that means I need to talk to my manager, put in two weeks notice, train a replacement...."

Then all of a sudden, you're fired. This is good, in a sense, because you can immediately move on to looking for a dream job rather than puttering about for several weeks. But it's very shocking, and it would be easy to assume your energy work was terrible. "I wanted a dream job, and now I have no job at all! I'm worse off!"

As another example, suppose Brianna has a mostly-3D-sort of life, but she really wants a fantastic romantic relationship. If she succeeds in connecting with 5D energy, she may discover that the "Hot Guys in Your Hood" app on her phone stops working. She can't get her trashy friends to hook her up on blind dates anymore. The restaurant she really liked to go on dates at closes. Now she's got *no* dates and *no* prospects. Things look even worse than they were before she started this 5D stuff! The 3D dating structures in her life are falling apart because they don't resonate with this new, joyful energy. They resonated with Brianna's 3D energy of disappointment, wilted flowers, and guys with bad breath.

If Brianna keeps up the 5D energy, new structures will begin to emerge. She might join a hobby club and make some new friends who set her up with better blind dates. She may find a dating app that doesn't feel so sleazy. She might start meeting new guys and hanging out with them.

Eventually, she'll get the relationship she wanted...but with a steady relationship in 5D, that 5D energy is likely to start affecting the *other* parts of her life. She may wind up losing her 3D-heavy job. She might have to move. Her old poor health habits may start causing bigger and bigger problems for her, because they just don't resonate with the energy she's playing with now. So now she has to change her health habits as well.

If Brianna knows she's just outgrowing old patterns, she can adapt to these changes more easily. If she reads the loss of 3D patterns as a bad thing, though, she might quit and try to go back to the way things were.

- **The advice may be correctly applied, and positive changes result. But because the new changes feel oh-so-good, the old patterns seem extra rotten by comparison. And now the person gets very judgy about those old patterns.** We need to have compassion when thinking about old patterns. Though they were often unpleasant and destructive, they were an experience of an energy that we were intentionally exploring. Once we move higher, the temptation can be to look down on who we were before and on those who are still stuck at that energy. For some people, the tendency is to beat up on themselves. "Why did I stay in that abusive job so long? How could I have been so egocentric and out of touch with my heart? What kind of person *was* I? I must have hurt myself and others so badly, for no good reason...." For others, the tendency is to preach to family members or even random strangers about how bad their 3D patterns are and how they need to "get Jesus" and go 5D. Either way, that judgy energy is usually 3D. It will pull you back down into 3D patterns--maybe not the same ones, but new judgy ones. (For more on the difference between judgment and judgyness, see the chapter called "Avoid Judgyness, Not Judgment.")

It might seem like a lot to have an entire chapter on what can go wrong with 5D advice, but I felt it was necessary. It's very easy for LOA teachers of high vibration to forget what life was like for people just starting out. In their defense, most of the people reading LOA books are in 4D and 5D in most areas of their lives, with just a few areas left in 3D. This makes selecting the right energy and handling unexpected outcomes much easier. So it's understandable that many authors don't feel the need to address what happens when their advice is applied in a largely-3D life.

But I do think it's worth saying that life is very different when you're mostly 3D. If you're a person with lots of 3D-level issues, then intense hard work, struggling, berating people, and controlling just *works* a lot better than 5D advice. It gets more things done. Not joyfully, and not very well, but it gets something done. When 3D people compare that to the mystifying 5D advice, it's no wonder they resist it and mock it as useless and delusional.

This is one truth a lot of LOA teachers overlook: the path of struggle really does get results for a lot of people. Many of us started out with most parts of our lives in 3D energy, and we can remember times when we worked very hard and it paid off. We don't want to ignore those times. We want to acknowledge that there was a time and place for that kind of energy and action. For most of us, we're moving beyond that in most areas of our lives, but it really did work for us in the past.

For one thing, the Earth back then was at a different place in her own planetary journey. When Mother Earth had mostly 3D energy, her vast, powerful energy supported 3D ideas and 3D solutions. Now she has evolved into 4D and will quickly shift into 5D, so different energies and solutions will be more supported. Our own personal energy plays a role in that evolution--we can hold her back or help her move faster. Right now, humankind as a group is hanging back in upper 3D energy, with many millions of human scouts forging ahead into 4D or 5D. 3D solutions are not going to work very well for long anymore. But there was a long period of time in human history where hard work and micromanaging were very good things.

Offering 5D tools to people with mostly 3D energy should be done cautiously. If you're reading this book, your energy is probably 4D or 5D overall, so you may not have many of the difficulties described here.

But if you decide to share these ideas and tools with others, do so with awareness. Make sure the person really understands that it's energy that really shifts circumstances, not the outward actions or the inner psychoanalysis. Make sure you can coach the person into the 5D energy state. And acknowledge that 5D energy is very powerful, and will not resonate with anything in their life that is 3D, so some things might change that they weren't expecting to change. These changes will be for the better...eventually. In the meantime, it can be a lot of chaos.

IF ALMOST ANY ACTION CAN BE TAKEN FROM ANY VIBRATION, HOW DO I KNOW WHICH ONE I'M USING?

I'd like to take a moment to really make something clear: almost any action, spiritual practice, or inner work can be done from any vibrational level.

From what I've said so far, you might assume that any outward action is 3D and any inner work is 4D. This is not true. Action, thought, and feeling can happen on any level of consciousness. It's not that "any action is 3D," but rather, the *preoccupation* with action is 3D. You can take outward action from any kind of energy. 3D is the fussy, insistent energy that claims action is the only thing that really matters.

Similarly, it's not that "any inner work is 4D." 4D is the *preoccupation* with inner work, the perspective that says inner work will save us all. People in 5D will still take outward action and may still do inner work. But they won't have the perspective that these things make the world go round. They will do inner and outer work when it's fun, because it's fun. Not because they are trying to get life to shape up.

Almost Any Action Can Be 3D, 4D, or 5D

Most actions can be taken with 3D, 4D, or 5D energy. The exception are actions that by their nature involve violating someone's free will. Murder, rape, fraud, and other actions that by definition involve violating the free will of another are always 3D. The energy of dishonoring another is always a low vibration.

That said, any other sort of action could be combined with 3D, 4D, or 5D energy. The fact that you're doing yoga, for example, doesn't by itself indicate whether you're using 3D, 4D, or 5D energy. You could do your taxes, pray, or sip a slushie each in a 3D, 4D, or 5D way. It's the energy in the action that matters.

Let's take the yoga example deeper. You might start out doing yoga just as a way to get strong, look hot, be healthy, and impress people. You might work hard on it and force yourself to get up early to practice. Your motives would tend to focus on how yoga will improve your social standing, your longevity, and your strength. This would be a fairly 3D experience.

With time, you might discover that the movements of yoga help you understand your body in a new way. You might notice how you feel calmer and have clearer thoughts afterwards, and want to duplicate that experience. So you start doing yoga with more focus and more discipline, trying to develop a routine that produces that output of calm feelings, clear thinking, and a strong body awareness. Your motives shift to self-improvement as a soul. This would be a fairly 4D experience.

As you develop further in your practice, you may notice something happening *underneath* all the calm feelings and stretching muscles. You might sense a flow of energy that moves in interesting ways, and become fascinated with playing with that energy as you move. You might continue the same routine, or you might find yourself moving more spontaneously, just playing with how things feel.

At first, a routine might help you connect with the energy

better, but with time you may realize you don't even need a routine. The energy is always there, and your soul is always in touch with it, whether there's a routine or not. You don't care whether you're getting to be a yoga expert anymore.

You're not very interested in doing yoga "to be a better person," because this energy is just fun, and you have a sneaking suspicion you're just fine as you are. One time-slice of you isn't better than some other time-slice of you. The 2023-yoga-expert-you isn't better or more worthy than the 2019-yoga-slouch-you.

Sometimes it's fun to practice a difficult pose again and again until you get it, but it's about the fun of the challenge, not trying to be a better person. Your motives are about fun, play, and love. This would be a fairly 5D experience.

Of course, in real life our energies mix all the time. That's why I describe these scenarios and say they are "fairly" 3D, 4D, or 5D. There's usually a mix of vibrations going on for each of us, depending on the day and the activity. And it's difficult to encapsulate which energy is which with verbal descriptions and generalizations. It's always the energy underneath that matters, not other things. But what if you're having trouble sensing which energy is there? In that case, a few generalizations may help, even though they won't be absolutely perfect guidance. That said, here's my attempt at generalizing energy in terms of motives and experience:

You're usually doing an activity mostly in 3D if your motives are focused on changing the external world and your experience is one of heavy struggle, overcomplication, and unpleasantness.

You're usually doing an activity mostly in 4D if your motives are focused on changing yourself and your experience is one of light, occasional struggle, mild confusion, and fairly good feelings.

You're usually doing an activity mostly in 5D if your motives are focused on just having fun or just loving (rather than changing anything) and your experience is joyful, easy, or challenging in an enjoyable way.

Now of course, we usually have more than one motive. That's why I say it matters whether your motives are *focused* on, say, external approval, or just happen to include external approval as an afterthought. You might be doing an activity mainly for the fun of it, while also being glad that other people like what you're doing--like painting a picture for the fun of it, but also being glad if it sells or makes your hubby smile. It's okay to have mixed motives. The question is which motives are primary.

To find out which motives are primary, you can just pose some hypotheticals to yourself. In the painting example, we could ask, "If this painting didn't sell, how much would that matter to you? Would you feel like painting it wasn't worth the time? Would you wish you had done something else? Would you rather paint something that's boring to you but that sold for a lot of money?" Hypotheticals like these tease out how much force different motives have for you.

For the yoga example, we could ask, "If it turned out that science proved yoga didn't help your body at all and didn't make you any healthier, would you still do it? If everyone in your yoga class thought you were lousy at yoga, how much would that matter to you? If you had to choose between a yoga class that wasn't much fun but gave great results in self-control, or a yoga class that was tons of fun but didn't cause improvements in self-control, which would you pick?"

There is a lot of nuance to all these ideas about energy. It's always the energy underneath that matters, not the action, thought, emotion, body sensation, or motive. But in case you have difficulty sensing the energy, I wanted to use this chapter as a chance to home in on what the kinds of energy are like a little bit more.

Now let's get to the methods for shifting to 5D.

HOW TO SHIFT TO 5D

We've talked a lot about how important energy is, and how 3D patterns are usually at the bottom of the irritating, unsatisfying parts of your life. But how are you supposed to shift those 3D patterns? How do you invoke the higher vibrational energy that can disrupt the old junk and swing you into the new life you love?

There are already a multitude of books on how to shift to 4D. Usually, authors won't describe it in that language. Instead, they'll call it "shadow work," "psychotherapy," "inner child contact," "mindfulness," "ritual casting," "body work," or some other modality that puts a lot of attention on changing your life by changing your mind, emotions, or body awareness. Because you can find so much of this advice elsewhere, I'm not going to bother with rehashing how to shift to 4D here. The main lesson of 4D is "monitor and adjust what you are thinking and feeling and get in touch with your body."

Instead, I'm more interested in how to shift to 5D. Shifting to 5D is an energetic step. It's hard to talk about energy because we don't yet have a good vocabulary for it, but it's worth the effort because 5D energy will change your life much more powerfully and much more quickly than 4D. So I'll do my best to express it in words. I invite other mavericks to create new language for describing all this, and new methods that will work even better than these! There is still much for energy workers to contribute in the exploration of 5D.

So far as I can tell, there are four main ways to shift to 5D energy:

1. Ask for help from higher beings.

2. Connect 5D energy from one area of your life (one that's working well) to the problem area.

3. Shift the energy of the problem area directly, using a particular energetic attitude of openness.

4. Radiate your signature vibration. This method is too detailed a topic for this book, so it will come in a later book.

I'll address the first two options in this chapter, and give separate, in-depth chapters for #3.

Shifting to 5D by Asking for Help

At first, I wanted to brush off this method as of little help. But consistently over time, asking for assistance from the divine, angels, the Fae, nature spirits, ancestor spirits, Ascended Masters, spirit guides, or whatever being you believe to be of substantially higher vibration than yourself *has proven vital.*

Although we can shift energy directly ourselves, it can be awfully hard to actually do that when we're really hurting. Instead, asking an entity of higher love and consciousness to assist you in shifting your vibration can help you get out of the muck and into a space where you can make your own choices more freely.

How do you ask for help? Energetic tools are tools of intention, so there's no complicated system. You just decide who it is you're asking and intend letting them know you want vibrational assistance to shift higher.

You can put this into words if you want to, but it's not necessary. An example might be, "Mother Mary, help me shift my vibration higher." Or, "Fairies, help me align with my best vibration." Or, "Thank you, angels, for always helping me be high-vibrational."

Of course, you could ask for help that's more specific to your situation as well. "Angels, please get this bill paid." That might or might not happen, because often the beings we're appealing to have limited access to 3D stuff and are not as good at shuffling material objects around, getting you through traffic swiftly, or blowing hurricanes off-path. And they will typically not interfere with the free will choices of others, so if what you want depends on that, they may not help the way you've asked. That's not to say higher beings will never help with these things. Specific practical requests might still work; it's just a little more hit-or-miss.

Higher-dimensional beings tend to understand a lot about cause and effect, and which choices now might produce good results later. They're less good at understanding *how hard* such choices are for those of us living on Planet Earth.

They can see that negativity is bad. They may even remember it being bad from past lives. But when you're immersed in the high vibrations and love of the Other Side, the badness just doesn't seem as problematic.

Here's what my guides said about it:

Those of us on the Other Side are much better able to see relationships and consequences, but we don't always know how things feel, nor how the feel of things can be distracting, alienating, disturbing, reassuring, and so on. Your feelings get in the way of your manifestations or amplify them, and we can't always predict that part because we don't feel it to the same degree. We still have feelings here, but we are immersed in a love so grand that it's hard to get upset in the way Earthlings get upset. We are always so aware of the bigger picture.

Here's a metaphor that may help. Suppose there are two little children who each want to watch the same scary movie, *DeathSchool 2*. One of them, Jeremy, watches the movie at home late at night while his parents are out. The house is empty, a thunderstorm is rattling the windows, and Jeremy is all alone. He watches the whole movie in one sitting, biting his nails the whole time and jumping at shadows. The movie seems very, very scary!

The other kid, Marie, happens to watch the same movie, but in the middle of a sunny day. Broad daylight is streaming in, and the scent of hot chocolate is filling the air. Marie is sitting on her mother's lap as she watches, and her mother is stroking her hair and saying calming things. Her brothers are wrestling and laughing on the floor near the screen, and sometimes their laughter is so loud Marie has to stop the movie and wait a while before turning it on again. Marie gets the movie in little bits, with lots of fun and laughter between each bit, and even at the scary parts she feels immersed in her family's support and comfort. *DeathSchool 2* is a scary movie--Marie can see that--but it doesn't seem that bad.

For us on Earth, we are like Jeremy. We are in the midst of negativity in an environment that does not support us very well. We feel alone. We often can't sense our angels or guides, and the scary scenes of our lives are usually things we can't take a break from. We just have to live them straight through.

For higher-dimensional beings, the scary movie of Earth is experienced more in the way Marie experienced it. They can see that bad things are happening, and they acknowledge there is negativity and hardship. But immersed in the light, fully aware of the love of the divine, those troublesome events on Earth don't seem *that* bad.

They may give very good advice and feel puzzled why we can't seem to take it, just as Marie might say, "If you start to get scared watching a scary movie, Jeremy, why don't you just imagine your mom holding you and telling you it will be all right?" For Marie, that's easy advice. For Jeremy, that might be quite difficult in a dark, empty house! Marie might feel puzzled why Jeremy won't just hop into that more loving, calm state.

Of course by now, most higher-dimensional beings understand that they tend to underestimate how difficult negativity is to handle emotionally on Earth, and so they tend to be more patient and give us smaller baby steps these days. But there still is a bit of a disconnect sometimes in their advice, and you may need to remind your angels, fairies, and so on to break action steps and ideas down to be as easy as possible!

As we've seen, higher-dimensional beings have a lot of hurdles in giving you physical help. But giving energetic help is their specialty. They are all about high vibrations! Assisting you in dissolving 3D energetic patterns and attuning you to 5D is much easier for them than practical to-dos. And since it's mostly your energy state that determines what happens in your life, helping you shift *that* is helping you with everything else, anyway!

(Why do I say it's only "mostly" your energy state that creates your life? Because others are making different choices with their free will, and we have agreed to allow others to have some influence on our lives. We have agreed they can create in our life. So it's *mostly* our energy state, *partly* other people's energy states, that create our lives.)

Asking for energetic help is powerful, and it's one of the few things that are easy to do when you're particularly angry, depressed, or otherwise struggling. So please don't overlook this 5D tool.

Shifting to 5D by Spreading 5D Energy from One Area to Another

As was said earlier, even if you sit on your butt and never make any further high-vibrational efforts, any 5D energy in your life will gradually begin affecting and reshaping the other areas of your life. The process is very slow if you do nothing to help it along, though. So one method we have for increasing the 5D energy in our lives is to notice where we already have 5D energy and tap into that a little as we consider our problematic, 3D patterns.

Nearly everyone reading this book has areas of their life that are already in 5D. They may be very tiny slivers of experience, like the energy underneath "listening to that one very happy song that makes me feel awesome," or "baking pistachio cookies," but if you've been in the woo-woo world for long, you've got them.

Probably most people on Earth have had at least a little 5D energy in their lives. For one person, it's the charmed life they lead in going to concerts--somehow it always works out that they get amazing seats and an unforgettable experience, with no real effort involved. For someone else, it's the ease with which they doodle, just having fun on paper with no expectations or judgyness. You may even have a larger aspect of life that is pretty well aligned with 5D--physical safety in your hometown, stable and enjoyable finances, or magnificent health.

Whatever the area, connect the energy you feel associated with that to the area you're having problems in. How do you do this? As you experience areas of your life that are fun and working well, feel into the energy a little more and remind yourself that your problem area can feel this way. That's all. Just consciously touch on your problem as you're feeling that flowing 5D in your baking, doodling, or robot-building, and remind yourself that the 5D energy is spreading to your problem area.

If you'd like a motivational boost, it helps to remember that Planet Earth is shifting quickly towards 5D and is already supporting movement in that direction. Mother Earth will help strengthen the 5D patterns you've got and loosen the old 3D stuff.

Not only that, but other people are working on the same patterns you have. If you're struggling with a sister relationship, there are many other people on Earth also working on healing 3D sister patterns. As you make tiny shifts, you help them. And as they work on expanding 5D into their sisterhoods (whether consciously as a woo-woo lightworker, or unconsciously as a so-called "muggle"), they create energetic pathways that you can follow.

This means that we are all making things easier for each other. The only thing that will *not* be getting easier and easier is keeping 3D patterns long-term! If that's your goal, you may have to leave Planet Earth to do that.

So far we've covered two 5D tools, asking for help shifting to 5D, and spreading 5D energy from one part of your life to another. Now it's time to turn to another 5D tool: energetic openness.

SHIFTING TO 5D WITH ENERGETIC OPENNESS

You can shift the energy of a stuck 3D pattern directly, using 5D energy of a particular kind. To do this, you need an energy that is high-vibrational, yet not such a stretch that it's too hard to get into. I call this an "open" energetic state.

Open 5D energetic states work because awareness is transformative. Just by applying 5D energy to the situation at hand, you subtly shift it at an energetic level. It usually takes a little time for the changes to show up in your emotions, and even longer to show up in the physical world. But having some relief at the energetic level still feels great, and you receive those benefits immediately!

What is an open state like? It looks different for different people. You want a state that observes the 3D pattern without resisting it. It has to somehow connect with the 3D pattern through your attention, and yet not get mired in the tired, dismal 3D energy. Different attitudes do this in slightly different ways.

Many of the open states are associated with an emotional flavor, but remember that it is not really the emotion that is important; it's the energy underneath. That said, here are five different open states you can try out:

1. Curiosity. This is the default, old stand-by path used both in LOA circles and mindfulness circles. The idea is to approach the 3D pattern you're interested in changing with a soft, receptive, observant sort of energy. Emotionally, many people describe this as being similar to curiosity.

For example, if you have big medical bills that just keep coming, you might try to lightly focus on the bills while entering a questioning, open state.

For some people, this translates to a certain kind of thinking ("I wonder where all this frustration about these bills is coming from" "What exactly is it like, this feeling of having too many bills?") or a certain kind of feeling (curiosity, puzzlement, interest). But again, it's not really the thinking or the feeling that is doing the work. It's the energy underneath it all. Many people just associate it with certain thoughts and feelings and have an easier time connecting with that soft, open energy by using those thoughts and feelings.

It's important to note that in this and any other "open" state, you are connecting with the low-vibrational pattern without getting judgy about it. You're not pushing the bills away or fussing at them. You're just observing them and whatever comes up inside you.

Those using a 4D perspective will lean heavily on the thoughts and feelings you have in your curious state. "Be sure to ask questions! Be sure to *feel* curious!" Those using a 5D approach will pay more attention to the energy directly.

2. Wonder. I am indebted to Alain Herriott, Jody Herriott, and Tyler Odysseus and their book *Energy Healing and the Art of Awakening through Wonder* for this practice. They advocate using a breathing technique that combines approaching your problem situation with a feeling of wonder. Although I think it's the energy underneath the wonder that really matters, focusing on the sensation of wonder helps many get into the right energetic state.

Think of something that makes you feel awe and wonder, such as the night sky, an exciting foreign city, or an immense ocean. Whatever you choose, focus on that and bring yourself into an open state, one that reaches out in an exploring way.

Then bring to mind your problem situation. Keep shifting back and forth between the feeling of wonder and the problem.

This energetic state and the emotional "flavor" associated with wonder is a little more emotional than curiosity. This may appeal to you, or you may prefer the more detached version in curiosity.

3. Trust. For decades, I found trust the most perplexing and frustrating idea in religion. Many people would advise me to trust God to take care of my problems, or to trust the universe that I would get what I wanted. I would say that I didn't believe things would work out well, and they would say, "Just trust that God will handle it." Um...how? How do you go from believing one thing is likely to believing the opposite is likely, just like that?

I would think, "I have to start believing that God or the universe will pay my phone bill somehow. But what evidence do I have for that? I guess I'm supposed to make myself believe it without any evidence, or repeat the few flimsy pieces of evidence I can drum up. Hmm, I don't seem to believe it, really, even after all that." It is very, very difficult to just *make* yourself believe something.

Luckily, trust does not require that. That's because trust is not a belief. It does not mean believing that God will make things okay. It does not mean you go from feeling scared to feeling confident. Trust is not a belief. It is not a feeling of confidence. It is an energy we step into. We can hold that energy even when we think we're doomed and feel scared and uncertain.

To me, the energy of trust feels both relaxing and sort of vulnerable, like stepping down onto something that shakes a little, or pulling down a wall that was blocking out something. It may feel different for you.

When you step into trust, you do it a tiny bit at a time. Don't try to suddenly believe with 100% certainty that your phone bill will be taken care of. That won't work.

Instead, move energetically into your own sensation of

trust, and tell yourself, "I'm going to trust a tiny bit about the phone bill. It's not like I think it's 100% sure that it's going to work out. I'm not even 50% sure. I'm just increasing my trust one tiny, tiny drop. I'm 0.001% more open to the idea that God will take care of it. That's it. I don't have any more trust than that. I'm just the teeniest bit more open."

You probably won't be able to hold this energy for very long. You'll get distracted by other things, and then the worry will pop up again. That's okay. Later, try to re-engage with trust energy again, and see if you can trust another tiny drop. "I still don't think it's likely things will be okay, but I'm going to trust one teensy bit more. Maybe there's a 1% chance the universe will get the bill paid. Maybe. I'm not sure, but I'm a little bit open to the idea."

You might think, "Goodness, it's going to take forever to get to 100%!" In my experience, you don't need to get anywhere near 100% trust. Often 1% or 5% is plenty. Somehow, the energy of trust is much more powerful than our conscious evaluation of our beliefs. With trust energy, you can still be thinking thoughts like "It's 95% likely my phone will be shut off" and yet get happy results.

Your mind is trying to scan the world and figure out what's likely, but it usually doesn't take much notice of the energy underneath things, even though it's energy running the show.

That's why your mind keeps saying, "Nope, probably still going to get my phone shut off" even as things are shifting powerfully at the energetic level. That's okay. You don't need to believe something you don't believe. You don't need to feel confident. The energy of trust is a radical change-producer, and it will sort things out despite your bad beliefs and crummy emotions. All you have to do is keep connecting with it in tiny ways, when you can remember to. Keep practicing stepping into your version of trust, and see what happens.

4. Surrender. Surrender is a similar energy to trust, but it is a much more powerful, much more open sort of energy.

Instead of dropping down onto a shaky step, you are falling into a void. Instead of pulling down one wall, you are laying waste to everything. (As always, find your own metaphors and language for your energetic states, but this is what it feels like to me.)

I find it too difficult to achieve this state when I am worried about something, but many, many people describe it as pivotal to their spiritual life. It's worth trying out if you can manage it.

5. Humor. For many people, finding a way to laugh at a bad situation shifts the whole energy around it. Instead of attacking or resisting it, it just loosens up the energy or throws it all up into the air entirely (in a way similar to surrender, oddly enough).

For example, if your phone bill arrives and is much too high, you might declare, "This is clearly the work of my archenemy, PriceyMobile. They mean to crush my spirit entirely with their evil. Well, they win! I will walk into their vampire den and let them feed on the blood of my smartphone.....But the legacy of my sacrifice shall live on...." Or you stick out your tongue at the email and consider the phone company properly decimated. "Didn't think I could do that to you, did you? Bet you're sorry now!" Or you say something that makes no sense yet feels oddly satisfying. "Ridiculous phone bill? Well, now they owe me a teacup."

If you can manage it, humor can shift energetic states in a hurry. It can be hard to find the wherewithal to take this attitude in hard times, though emergency room nurses, soldiers, and others learn to practice a "dark humor" that helps them stay energetically afloat in life-threatening situations. If curiosity and trust feel sappy or dull to you, humor may be more your style in shifting energy.

There are two things to keep in mind if you decide to use humor as an open state. The first is to ensure that the energy around your humor is genuinely open and high. Bitter jokes and sarcasm that puts you down may swing you deeper into 3D. It's the energy underneath that matters, as always. Does your humor make you feel uplifted? Does it feel like genuine relief, or an extra stab of unpleasantness or resentment?

The second thing to remember is to make sure you connect your humor to the bad situation you want to shift. Laughing about something unrelated feels good, but doesn't necessarily lift the vibration of the problematic 3D pattern. Getting distracted by something funny but off-topic may give you some relief but not really address how you're flowing energy to your particular problem. Bring your humor *to* the problem, in a way that feels uplifting to you.

Caveats about Energetic Openness

To be clear, I'm not saying that all cases of curiosity, wonder, trust, surrender, and humor are 5D. Sometimes people have emotional states like these but lousy 3D energy or internally-analytical 4D energy underneath.

As always, the important thing is the energy, but because it's awkward talking about energy directly, we have to wind our way around it with a lot of other terms. Test out for yourself what kinds of curiosity feel high-vibrational and what kinds feel 3D. When does humor feel open and expansive, and when does it feel malicious and constricted? Find out what states work for you.

There are other open states that you can explore. They are described in different ways depending on the person: "radically accepting," "leaning in to a situation," "allowing," "peace," and so on. Whichever state you choose, it needs to feel energetically open, smooth, free (insert your descriptive word of choice from the "Sensing Energy" chapter), but not so high that you can't experience it in a tough moment.

Matt Kahn suggests using love as the state of energy for such things ("Whatever arises, love that"), but for many people, it's too hard to get into a loving energetic state when poop has hit the fan. In the next chapter, I'll give a more specific, optional walkthrough for using the open state of peacemaking or love, if that resonates with you. If you are able to get into the energetic states correlating to love, joy, power, and so on, by all means do so, but don't be hard on yourself if you can't jump that high when you're thinking about your broken-down car or your ex.

Whichever open state you choose, you're bringing 5D energy to a 3D pattern. Struggling with the 3D pattern is just more 3D energy: struggle, hardship, resistance. That's why it's so important to find a state that doesn't feel like you're resisting or pushing against the bad situation. If you struggle against it, you at best just get a different stuck pattern, a different 3D problem.

5D is the energy of receptivity. It just allows everything to be. That doesn't mean you have to resign yourself to liking the problem or putting up with it. It just means you don't get judgy about it. Instead of declaring, "This crazy phone bill simply OUGHT NOT BE!" you have more of the attitude of, "This bill is really not my thing. I think I'll change it."

Experience the 3D energy and the higher-dimensional awareness (the energetically open state) at the same time. Shift into a tiny bit of trust, wonder, humor, curiosity, or surrender in the midst of your turmoil. Even a tiny bit will have good effects.

AN EXAMPLE PROCESS OF ENERGETIC OPENNESS: HOW TO MAKE PEACE WITH EVENTS AND FORGIVE PEOPLE

This is a step-by-step explanation of using love or peace as an energetically open state to face a problematic event or person. It is also a method of forgiveness, if you choose for it to be.

There are many books and seminars on forgiveness and making peace with life. You have probably already heard the basics: that forgiving someone doesn't mean condoning what they did, that holding on to a grudge hurts you rather than them, that making peace with a tough situation can be a first step to leaving it. (For example, it's often said that until you find happiness in a single life, you won't attract a good relationship.) There is less said about exactly *how* to go about forgiving someone or making your peace with a situation. How do you connect the energy of peace with a 3D pattern?

Before I go into a step-by-step how, I'd like to point out

that pushing yourself to forgive or make peace is not good. Check your intuition and make sure that now really is the time to forgive or accept a situation.

Studies show that forgiveness usually isn't experienced as a particular, direct event. Instead, most people just "discover" that they have already forgiven. There's often no shining, teary moment of forgiving. Instead, people simply look back (after days, months, or years) and realize that somewhere along the way, they forgave what happened. So if you're not feeling led to forgive in this moment, that's not really a problem. Probably it will happen on its own, without effort, as you progress in life.

Pushing yourself to forgive or accept, on the other hand, is toxic. It's a form of spiritual bypassing. We resist forgiveness or making peace when our emotions haven't yet had their full say.

Anger continues its message of "What happened to me hurt, and that matters!" until you really, truly, deeply get it. Trying to cut that short usually means the anger pops back up again later, because you haven't yet internalized how much your feelings matter in life.

Similar things happen with jealousy, sadness, and other feelings you might be tempted to bypass so you can hurry up and be a good little spiritual person. *Pushing yourself to forgive before you're ready does not make you a better person. It just short-circuits what you are trying to internalize and learn.*

That said, if you're getting the intuition that now is the time to work on forgiveness or making peace with a situation, you can proceed with the instructions. I'll use the terms "forgive the person" and "make peace with the situation," but this can work for anything you want to come to terms with--an event, a person, a disease, whatever. You can forgive the shark who bit off your toes, if you feel called to do so, even though a shark isn't a person or a situation.

In the instructions, I'll ask you to imagine some things about God/Source/the Universe/divine love/whatever. You can insert any term that resonates for you, so long as the entity is very loving, preferably all-loving. I'll use "the Divine," but feel free to substitute what works for you.

The process involves a series of questions that you answer as honestly as possible. There is no judgment for any answer. Don't try to give a "spiritually correct" answer, give an honest answer.

How to Forgive a Person or Make Peace with a Situation:

1. Bring the person or situation to mind. Next, suppose that the Divine is standing by, full of love, ready to love the problematic person or situation but not yet doing so. You can forbid the Divine to love this person or situation. You can tell the Divine not to love them if you want to. Or, you can give permission for the Divine to love them. If you give permission, you're not saying <u>you</u> love the person or situation in any way. It has nothing to do with you personally. You're not being asked to do anything for them, or feel anything for them, or say anything to them. You don't have to love them even a teeny tiny bit. You're just deciding whether *the Divine* is allowed to love them. (Obviously, we don't really have the power to forbid God or whatever to love anyone, but for the sake of the thought experiment, pretend you can. And know that the Divine will love you no matter what you choose.)

Are you willing for the Divine to love this person or situation?

If so, breathe that permission in. Acknowledge that it's okay for the all-loving Divine to love this troublesome situation or person. You don't have to do anything. You're just giving permission for the Divine to do its thing. (This sensation of *giving the permission to love* is the energetic sensation that builds the energetic state. It is a 5D intention. It will increase as we go along.) If you've breathed in and given permission for the Divine to love them, go on to Step 2.

If you're not willing to give that permission, that's okay. Your emotions are signalling you that they haven't had enough time to say what they need to say. Take some time off from intensive spiritual work and just play, relax, and go about your regular business. In a few days or weeks, you may feel like trying again. Or you may find you forgive without needing a process. Let whatever happens be okay for a while.

2. Next, imagine that the Divine could send love *through you* as a conduit, if you are willing, to the situation or person. This does not mean that you personally will love the person or situation. You may still hate their guts, personally. But you can decide to give or withhold permission for the Divine to use you as an energetic channel for the Divine's love to come to this person or situation. You won't have to take any action. You won't have to feel any differently about them. This will take no effort and no emotion on your part. You would just be like an empty tunnel for love to move through you, *from* the Divine *to* the person or situation.

Are you willing to let the Divine flow love to this person or situation through you as a conduit?

If so, breathe that permission in. Let yourself open up energetically. You do not have to start liking the person. You do not have to start feeling better about the situation. All you have to do is open and allow the Divine to start flowing love *through* you. You are just a hollow reed for the love to pass through. After a few moments of being the conduit, move to Step 3.

If you're not willing to be a conduit, again, that's okay. Your emotions need more time to integrate. Don't push yourself further into the process. Just take a break and come back to it later, if you feel called to.

3. Next, imagine that as the Divine is flowing its love through you, it could also stimulate a teeny, tiny bit of your own love to join it and bless this person or situation. This would be a very, very small amount of love--say, 0.01% of your capacity, or smaller if you wish. The Divine could help a tiny trickle of your own love to move with divine love towards this person or situation. It could be one tiny drop of your love. It does not mean you have to go hang out with that person, or that you have to live in the crappy circumstance with a smile on your face, or anything like that. It is just about one tiny drop of love.

Are you willing to let the Divine stimulate love from you as it flows love toward this person or situation? Are you willing for one tiny drop of your love to bless this person or situation?

If so, breathe in that willingness. Allow a very, very small amount of love to flow from you. It joins the greater flow of the love of the Divine and moves toward that person or situation. Feel this for as long as feels comfortable. You may need to take a break and do something else before going on to Step 4. That's okay.

If you're unwilling for even a tiny drop of your own love to go to this person or situation, that's okay. There's no judgment. It just means you need more time to honor your own feelings about all this. You have been hurt deeply, and it takes time to integrate that. Take a few days or weeks off from intensive spiritual work, and just relax and enjoy life as best you can. Give yourself whatever self-care seems appropriate. Then, if you feel called to, you can come back to the process. You can start from the beginning, or pick up at Step 3, whichever you prefer.

4. Once you're willing for a teeny, tiny bit of your own love to flow towards this person, see if you are willing to allow the Divine to help you increase the amount. If you gave one drop of love, are you willing to give two or three? If you offered 0.01% of your love, would you be willing to increase that to 0.05%, or even 1%?

Breathing slowly, gradually increase the amount as far as you are willing, making the increases in tiny chunks if you need to. Again, there's no outward action you need to take. You don't need to go call up the person on the phone. You don't need to declare you're forever okay with the crummy situation. You're just shifting the amount of love you're flowing.

Are you willing to let the Divine help you increase the amount of love you give to this person or situation?

If so, keep increasing the amount until it starts feeling hard, and then back off a little. Flow whatever amount of love feels reasonably comfortable to you.

If you ever get to 100%, there's probably no particular

reason to keep doing the exercise for this person or situation. You don't actually need to get to 100% for real emotional shifts and forgiveness to happen, though. In my opinion, the moment you are willing for the Divine to flow love to them, even without you, that's forgiveness. That's Step 1! That's probably all the forgiveness that is really insisted upon in life. But most people don't feel comfortable enough moving on with life until they get to Step 4 at maybe 10% love. For emotional health, trying to get to 10% is a pretty good goal. Don't be too hard on yourself and insist only 100% love counts. This is a very negative world, and even the tiny success of moving to 1% love about someone or something you hate is a huge deal.

If you're not willing to let the Divine help you increase the amount of love, then again, take some time off and relax. Come back to it later if you feel led to.

If you want to feel more independent, you can add a Step 5, in which you leave the Divine out of the equation and see yourself as the source of love. "Seeing yourself as a source of love, are you willing to flow your love to this person or situation?" This isn't necessary, but it might appeal to those who want to explore themselves as a source of love. In reality, we never have to be the sole instigator of love because we are always connected to the divine, and the divine is always flowing love. But if you'd like to, feel yourself as a source of love and try flowing that.

The key point of forgiveness or making peace is moving from a state of pure resistance to the tiniest willingness for goodness or love to bless that person or situation. That shift is the one that matters most, energetically. Any progress you make in flowing more and more love to them is just wonderful icing on the cake. That will help your manifestations move more smoothly, but the real energetic win requires much less.

When you move from a state of constricted energy to the teeniest, tiniest flow, that flow will eventually unwind everything related that is stuck. A bigger flow means the unwinding happens faster, but you don't have to go fast. You can consciously work on successfully completing Step 1 and then let the natural process handle the rest, if you're not in a hurry.

One reason this process is helpful is that seeing the flow of love as something outside of yourself takes the pressure off. When you're considering whether God or the universe should love that mean guy who got you fired, you don't feel like you have to be saintly and somehow make yourself love the jerk.

Sometimes it's easier to see love as something external we align with at first. I know, I know--a million self-help and spiritual books declare over and over that "all love is within you." That's true in a sense, but it's just a lot of pressure when you're being your normal human self trying to handle a setback. Let God, Goddess, Mother Earth, nature, the universe, or whatever do the loving work at first, and then join in when you're ready. This eases you into the right energetic state instead of starting you out with a ton of resistance.

AVOID JUDGYNESS, NOT JUDGMENT

We've looked at several methods for bringing in 5D energy--asking for help from nonphysical beings, engaging in an activity that already helps us feel 5D and then spreading that energy to our problem, and taking an energetically open stance like surrender, humor, trust, curiosity, wonder, love, or peace. These are things to start doing.

There are also two things to stop doing, if you want more 5D energy. You stop being judgy (that's covered in this chapter) and you stop bullying yourself (covered in "Don't Bully Yourself").

It is sometimes said that the key feature of a spiritual life is nonjudgment. On this view, spiritual growth is a process of moving from being deeply judging about life to judging less and less until you reach a point of nonjudgment about all things.

This whole idea confused me a lot until I realized that the way judgment is typically described--as a cognitive thing, a thought--is not the kind of judgment actually at issue. Judgment is not mentally labelling things. Judgment is (surprise, surprise) an energy.

When I first heard about being nonjudgmental, I thought the goal was no longer to have thoughts that labelled things as good or bad. But this is not the goal--in fact, this is not even a beneficial thing. Labelling things as good, bad, pleasant, unpleasant, desirable, undesirable, preferable, unpreferred, and so on is perfectly normal and adaptive. It helps steer you in life.

But when I first started thinking about the topic, I thought any kind of mental labelling was bad, and that made me very confused. "Should I hang out with this person? She's a thief. No, wait, I can't call her a 'thief.' That's judging her. Maybe she had good reasons for taking that guy's wallet. No, wait, I can't call anyone's reasons 'good' or 'bad'--that's judging, right? Oh, dear! I'm not doing this very well. And now I'm judging myself for being judgmental! Ack!"

You can call mental labelling "judgment" if you wish, but it's not the kind of judgment that we are trying to avoid as we grow in love and rise in vibration. Mentally labelling axe murderers as dangerous and axe murder as bad is helpful. It's a way of guiding behavior.

Trying to make yourself pretend that you are as delighted with axe murder as you are with fuzzy puppies is ridiculous. Of course you have a preference--and it's a very strong preference! Fuzzy puppies inspire love (at least for a lot of us), while axe murder is not very conducive to love.

There's a certain kind of love (unconditional love) that treats everything the same, everything equally worthy of love. We have that, but we also have a human perspective that makes some things good for us (food, love, safety, huggable puppies) and other things bad for us (starvation, hate, danger, axes stuck in us). Mental labels are very helpful for our human perspective.

So if we are trying to learn not to judge, and judging isn't mental labelling, then what is it? Judgment is a certain kind of energy that underlies *some* mental labelling.

Because it's an energy, it's difficult to describe, and the words you choose to use for it may be different than mine. For me, it's a fussy, sticky sort of energy. It feels like a stringy spiderweb holding things stuck and getting whatever touches it stuck, too. For many it feels like there is an electric "charge" to the issue. It may feel a little different to you.

Whatever the energy sensation is for you, let's use a new term to differentiate it from "judgment" (a.k.a. mental labelling). I call it "judgyness." It's fine to judge; it's bad to be judgy.

It's perfectly fine to label things as good or bad or helpful or unhelpful. Where things go wrong is when we don't just say something is good or bad, but also get "judgy" about it.

Pet peeves are things we notice in the world that we not only call bad, but tend to get "judgy" about. We don't just say they are bad and try to avoid them. We fill ourselves up with a fussy, insistent, buzzing sort of energy that tends to hold things in place. However it feels for you, it usually feels unpleasant compared to your happy shiny self.

Not only does judgy energy feel uncomfortable, but it tends to hold whatever we are getting judgy about in place energetically. On a physical level you might be moving away from that noisy neighbor, or that billboard with the bad grammar, or whatever other pet peeve is at work. On an energetic level, your judgy energy is holding it fast, locking it in for another go-round later.

We can contrast this with things that are bad that we *don't* get judgy about. Since which specific topics you are judgy about varies from person to person, I'll try and make up an example that hopefully applies to you. (If it doesn't, perhaps you can tweak it until it does.) Here goes:

You don't like lima bean flavored ice cream. Maybe you've never even eaten it before, but you hate lima beans and so it's fair to say you wouldn't like this ice cream either.

You don't like lima bean ice cream. If you saw it in an ice cream store, you wouldn't buy it. If someone filled your freezer with it, you'd throw it out. You don't want it. You find it gross. You avoid it. If someone force-fed you lima bean ice cream, you would experience it as a misfortune.

And yet, you probably are not judgy about lima bean ice cream. As you consider this example, you probably do not feel that same fussy, whiny, tense energy that you felt when you considered one of your pet peeves. Lima bean ice cream is gross, unappealing, and bad, but you're not all that upset about it just the same. If you were forced to eat it, you'd say, "Well, that stunk," and then move on with your life.

It's not that you're emotionless about it. You'd have some strong negative emotion while being force-fed lima bean ice cream. You really would hate it. It's just that there's no fussy, sticky energy underneath it, so even if the unpleasant thing happens, it's not a huge persistent drama. The negative emotion flows through you and dumps right out because energetically, there's nothing holding it to you. The negative emotion is just telling you that lima beans are gross, which you knew, and to avoid them, which you do as soon as you can, and that's that.

When you have judgy energy, negative emotions don't tell you something and leave. They get stuck. They keep telling you the same message over and over, and they spiral in on themselves.

That's when you find yourself yelling at your partner about how bowls go on the top rack of a dishwasher and anyone who does not do this is a cretin undeserving of love and romance. Deep down, you know it's a ridiculous thing to argue about. But with that judgy energy holding your annoyance in place, you can't move on. You get no relief from the annoyance so long as that bowl is still in the wrong spot and your partner still ignorant of the deep significance of its being in the wrong spot. Even if your partner hurries to put the bowl in the top and begs forgiveness, the annoyance lingers. It feels like the only way to let it go is to change the subject completely.

When you're judgy, negative emotions tend to get stuck in you, but if you're cold and emotionless, that cold and emotionless state can get stuck in your judgyness, too. It holds that in place as well. We've probably all run into someone who was talking in an extremely cold, indifferent way--and yet was chock-full of judgyness in their energy. Judgyness is not really about emotion, although a repeating emotion that seems overblown compared to the matter can sometimes be a sign judgyness is at work. What really matters is the energy.

So it's not about policing your thoughts to try to avoid "negative" thoughts. "That was a terrible restaurant. Oh, no! I can't say it is terrible. What a bad lightworker I am! Oh, no! I can't say that, either!" Negative labels are fine, so long as the energy underneath is not judgy. You can decide a restaurant is terrible without being judgy about it. Some people even find it hilarious when they find a terrible restaurant. It can become a source of fun. Or you can decide it was disgusting with a clear, empty energy, and you'll just move on with your life and go find a burrito bar you like better.

Liking and disliking sorts the universe for you. It steers you towards the things that resonate with your soul and away from the stuff that's not your role.

You are a piece of All-That-Is. As All-That-Is, unconditional love flows equally to all things. As a piece of All-That-Is, you can have that experience of unconditional love, and it's wonderful when you do.

But you also are a piece, an individual. As an individual with a limited perspective keyed to your kind of love (your soul), some things are better for you than others. From that perspective, liking and disliking are very useful. It can also be very fun to love and hate things. It's part of the Earth experience.

Where it gets less fun is when we don't notice what kind of energy is flowing through us underneath and we start sitting in sticky, fussy "judgy" energy. Then the things that annoy us just keep annoying us more and more, because we can't escape them in the long term. That judgy energy keeps them stuck in our energy field.

This can probably happen with more positive "judgy" feelings, like "I'm so much better than you because I recycled my bottle and you threw yours away." Then the emotion of self-righteousness gets stuck in us, which certainly feels better than misery or anger, but keeps us from moving into more joyful emotions. And underneath the veneer of emotion, the energy still feels sticky and fussy.

Hopefully at this point you understand that:
- We should indeed strive for "nonjudgment," but in the sense of "nonjudgyness" rather than policing thoughts.
- Judgyness is an energy underneath your emotions. If an

emotion seems particularly stuck in you, that may mean you have some judgyness, but judgyness is really about energy.

- Judgyness feels different to different people. Consider one of your pet peeves and explore the energy. Does it feel fussy? Stinging? Constricted? Stiff? Humming? Crackly? Once you know what it feels like, you know what to look out for.
- Judgyness holds things in place energetically. It is a function of your ego trying to keep you in dense, lower vibrations. When you choose to manifest something lighter and more joyful, you'll have to let go of whatever judgyness is associated with that topic. For spiritual advancement in general, address judgyness whenever it comes up.

Releasing Judgyness

So how exactly do you let go of judgyness? It is surprisingly easy, though it may have to be done several times on the same topic before you really clear it all.

When you sense that you are judgy about something, just focus on the judgy energy for a moment. Just sense it for twenty or thirty seconds, and it usually dissolves by itself. Remember, you're focusing on the energy *underneath*, not necessarily the topic that annoys you or the emotions you're having.

Just feel the fussy, insistent energy that is holding everything static like a spiderweb. You can say, "Hello, judgy energy," if that helps you focus.

How can it be this easy? For one thing, working on the energetic level tends to be faster and easier than working at the emotional or physical level.

But judgyness goes even farther in ease. Judgy energy just wants your attention. It's like a little kid who keeps tugging on his mom's jeans while she is busy. "Mom. Mom. Mom! Mom!! MOM!" He just tugs and says, "Mom!" over and over.

And then when she finally turns to him and says, "What?", he's got nothing to say!

He just looks sheepish and makes up something in a

hurry. "Um, I thought I saw a bug." Or just, "Hi, Mom."

As a bystander we might think this is pretty bizarre behavior, but when you're a kid, sometimes you just want your mom's attention for a nanosecond and then you're done. If you don't get her attention, the tension builds and things get crazy, but if you do, everything is peachy keen that instant. No long wait. No tedious process. That's all the kid wants: one moment of attention. And that's what your judgy energy wants, too.

To put it another way, judgy energy is relatively dense 3D energy. When you observe it directly without freaking out, you are using a higher vibration, usually 4D or 5D. The judgy energy is playing a role, helping anchor your ego in denser energies. It holds your energy in a particular pattern so that you stay on the same 3D vibrational level. But it is doing this to help you. It knows you came to Earth to experience 3D energies, of which it is one, and that it can help you stay grounded in the 3D realm for a longer "playtime."

When you observe it energetically, the higher dimensional energy you naturally bring to that observation tells the judgy energy you're ready to move on to a different experience. When you engage with that judgy energy neutrally, seeing it for what it is, it knows you're at a higher level of consciousness and that it's time to let go a little. It dissipates and lets other energies evolve and mature.

If the judgyness energy doesn't seem to budge for some reason or comes back, it helps to ask yourself, "How old does this energy pattern feel? Does it feel like I've felt this specific energy before?" You may notice that this particular judgy energy is a little different than the judgyness that came before. You thought it was the same stinging irritation you felt at your boss last week happening again, but on closer examination you realize this energy feels raspy, not stinging.

Or, you may realize it's an old energy that has been cycling in your life, appearing in a variety of situations and relationships. Then, seeing how this same old 3D pattern gets rehashed over and over helps you decide you're truly finished with it.

Either way, sometimes the extra attention examining the judgyness helps you realize you don't need this energy anymore and can let it go. The key is to spend most of your exploration of it on the way the energy feels, rather than on your thinking or the life situations around it. That helps the energy release and make room for higher vibrations.

Judgyness is not a bad thing. It's useful in keeping us in dense, low-vibrational existences, which we need to have the full Earth experience. But most of us are lightening up now and ready to move up to higher vibes, and that means the act of acknowledging and releasing our judy energy is a smart move for us.

But what if you really think someone is doing something destructive? Shouldn't you use judgyness to try and persuade them to stop? I asked my guides about this, and they said:

Judgment does not dissuade people from making harmful choices. It makes a person feel so bad they often recommit to harsh actions to justify themselves. The feeling of rejection is very strong. The question is, "How do I encourage this person to make a different choice without making them feel rejected?" That is a difficult task.

"So how do I do that?" I asked.

You affirm their belonging throughout the encounter, giving them love, and reduce the "judgy" nature of your complaint until you are just offering an alternative you think they will enjoy. If you do not think they will enjoy it, then you find new reasons for enjoyment in it, or you let the matter go.

"But what about protecting innocents?" I said. After all, I didn't want to abandon efforts to help innocent people who are at the mercy of bad guys.

You can take these efforts [like protecting innocents] *without judgyness, simply saying you do not want them to experience that and taking action.*

In other words, it's perfectly okay to decide that behavior like child abuse is not okay and to decide that the abuser should no longer have custody of the child. It's even okay to feel deeply angry or sad about the abuse.

What is less helpful is the fussy, insistent "judgy" energy that sometimes arises when we see something harmful. When we have that energy of judgyness or self-righteousness, then we are so harsh to the perpetrator that they tend to double down on their position. And then it's harder to find a solution, and the perpetrator seldom learns anything from the encounter, except that everyone seems to hate them and they need to defend themselves constantly.

Like what you like. Dislike what you dislike. Praise people for doing great things if you want to. Stop them from doing bad things if that seems appropriate. But whatever you decide to do, take the "judgyness" out of it.

DON'T BULLY
YOURSELF

The other thing to stop doing if you want to shift to 5D is to stop bullying yourself into being 5D all the time. Paradoxical, right?

Once we hear about a new way to improve our lives, it's common to get gung-ho and try to apply it all the time, and then judge ourselves for the times we fail to do so. If there's one consistent message in all the woo-woo sources I've heard, it's that the path to enlightenment, Ascension, happiness, what-have-you--is one of joy and ease. 5D energies are associated with joy, fun, ease, and effortless efforts.

Once you learn that choosing 5D energy is the main way to make your manifestations happen and live a happier life, you may find yourself trying to have 5D energy all the time. But sooner or later, this happens:

You run up against an old 3D pattern. A problem arises, it annoys you or scares you, and you feel awful.

Not only that, but now that you know more about how manifestation works, you know that your own choice of 3D energies is contributing to the problem!

And you know that choosing 5D energy instead would resolve things--instantly in the energetic realm, and with a bit of time in the physical realm. So what do you do? Continue to choose 3D energy, or make the new choice of 5D energy?

Intellectually, you know that 5D energy is wiser for getting you what you want. And from a cosmic perspective, you have ultimate free will. You can choose any kind of energy at any moment, from a cosmic point of view. You could choose 3D, or 2D, or 19D, or 5D, or anything, because your free will gives you opportunity to select any kind of energy to experiment with.

But in real Earthly life, it may not feel so easy to choose that high-flying 5D energy. The 3D energy changes which options feel realistic and accessible.

This is one reason why otherworldly angels, guides, and so on sometimes have a difficult time advising those of us on Earth. "Just choose the loving thing! There's a great option, right THERE. Just choose that! You can choose that at any moment," they might say.

But for us, that loving option might be clouded over, while 3D energy makes the "smash his rear windshield with a crowbar" option seem very obvious and natural. It can be tough for otherworldly advisors to know what to tell us! There are infinite options, but not all of them *appear* realistic or meaningful to us Earthlings.

3D patterns have struggle, strain, and hardship as their features. They make easy, wise solutions seem stupid or unrealistic. They make dumb, backfiring solutions look oddly reasonable. They warp you into perceiving 3D-level energies as oh-so-practical choices, even though those 3D energies just keep the problem going.

When you're enmeshed with a 3D pattern, you can still choose 5D energy, but the 5D choice may be hard to notice when you're in the midst of your drama. And even if you are made aware of it, such as from reading this book, that doesn't mean it will *feel* like a realistic choice in the moment.

Here's an example. I recently had a dumb 3D problem crop up. It was something small and nitpicky--I can't even remember what it was, because it was something so little--but it annoyed the heck out of me and made me feel a little depressed. From practicing with energy, I could sense directly how my own crummy 3D energy was adding to the problem and keeping it going. And I knew that if I shifted to 5D energy, the problem would eventually dissolve.

Sometimes, when a problem crops up, you can simply shift your choice to a higher level of energy, and that's that. In this case, I felt too frustrated and depressed to even make a 5D choice! "I know I'm a big contributor to this problem with my energy. I know changing my energy would fix it...but somehow, I don't want to. I feel pressured to be all goody-goody and do the 5D thing. And I don't want to. I just don't want to do anything."

I sat in that huffy, resistant energy for a while. I knew it was theoretically possible to make a 5D choice, but it just didn't seem reasonable in the moment. Then I remembered that I could ask my guides and angels to shift energy for me. Great news, right? But here's the kicker: *even asking for help seemed like too much trouble and stress!*

Talk about being mired in 3D energy! I was so enmeshed with the energy of struggle and strain that even asking for help from the angels seemed like too much work. It would have taken maybe five seconds of internal focus to intend, clearly and strongly, "Angels, help me shift to 5D choices. Make them easy for me." But those five seconds just felt like too much to ask. I sat in that 3D energy of angst and annoyance for another hour or two. (Yes, an *hour or two!*)

When I checked back in, the energy felt a little better, but I still felt stuck in 3D and didn't feel like shifting. I waited another hour or two, and at that point, I finally felt ready to make 5D choices. The resistance to being a "good little manifester" had finally eased off enough that I could just make a choice without feeling pressured or judged.

That's what to do if you encounter a problem and it just feels like too much to ask to shift to 5D: back off from trying, give yourself some space to whine in, and check in later to see if you feel able to shift then.

Why not push yourself to make the 5D choice as soon as possible? After all, all energetic choices are always available. You can make that choice sooner, theoretically, so why not strive for that?

Because if you bully yourself into trying for 5D energy, you can't actually reach 5D energy. The bullying is 3D energy, and 3D choices will never get you to 5D!

This is a huge difference from LOA models that say emotion or thought creates. If you think happy emotions create, you can bully yourself into producing the right neurochemicals for happiness. If you think positive thoughts create, you can bully yourself into thinking the right thoughts over and over.

But as you've probably learned from experience, happy emotions and positive thoughts don't do much creating in your life. It's the energy that creates, and you can't bully yourself into better energy. Bullying is pushy, clingy, sticky, 3D energy. It will never get you into free-flowing, high-vibrational 5D energy. They're just completely different.

Same with getting judgy with yourself about creating 3D problems. If you engage with judgy energy about how terrible you are for having 3D energy in the past that created some things you don't like, then that judgy energy goes on to create more 3D stuff. The harsher you are with yourself, the more 3D stuff is coming your way.

Berating yourself for mistakes just solidifies the 3D pattern you hate. Calling yourself names for manifesting things that bum you out just calls in more things that bum you out. Instead, you have to find an energetic perspective that acknowledges you did something you don't like the effects of *without* making yourself out to be some sort of manifesting villain.

And if you find it's too hard to stop judging yourself, you don't twirl your mustache and feel even *worse*. You just acknowledge, "Okay, then. I guess I'm judging myself for now." You stop the cycle of judging yourself for judging yourself for judging yourself. You just decide it's okay to have crappy energy for now.

When you push yourself to hurry up and have 5D energy, you've already lost. Pushiness isn't 5D, it's 3D. When you bully yourself into doing an activity that usually helps you feel a high vibration, guess what? It's unlikely to get you into that vibration that time. The energy of *I really need to do better and commit to all these 5D practices* is not a 5D energy. It's usually 4D if your focus is on self-improvement, 3D if you're hard-core hating on yourself.

When you get judgy with yourself for not trying to feel high vibrations this week, or not doing the gratitude practice your therapist suggested, or not doing the meditation Aunt Sally recommended, you're just continuing a 3D or 4D pattern that's unlikely to get you what you want. Instead, let it be okay that you're not "doing the things."

It's okay to have a crummy day. It's okay to let your practices slip. It's okay to back off from something and get some space and clarity about it.

3D patterns are part of the game of Earth, and you're not going to avoid them all. Instead of getting judgy with yourself for having problems, see if you can be gentle with yourself. We're all having a rough time on Planet Earth! Just being here is plenty of work. You're already enough. You've already done enough.

Problems come up, and we're not always in a space for transmuting them. If you're having a hard time, sometimes it's wise to just ride out the suffering. Obviously, if it feels okay to make a new energetic choice and select 5D, do that. But if feeling the energy of trust and acceptance or anything like that feels like too high a bar to reach right now, let that be okay. Back off from it. Don't bully yourself. You'll have a crummy time for a few hours, maybe even a few days, and then you'll check back and realize the 5D choice now feels accessible.

Although from a cosmic perspective, we have access to all energies at all times, Earth is designed to make slipping into negativity very easy and getting out a little more tricky. That's okay. That's part of what makes Earth an interesting place to be. We can explore negativity very thoroughly and very easily here. If it feels too hard to make a 5D choice right now, wait it out.

A time will come when the 5D choice feels reachable. You just have to check back periodically until that time comes. Ride the wave of crappiness for a while, knowing that you'll be able to step out of it when you're *truly* ready, not when your eager ego thinks you "ought" to be ready.

It sucks to ride out a wave of 3D energy and endure a problem, I know, but sometimes that's the better option--better than straining for an energy you can never get from strain, or getting down on yourself for getting down on yourself. A wise person waits for their moment.

In short, when a 3D pattern arises:

1. If you can do so without stress and drama, choose a 5D energy to home in on.

2. If that seems too hard, ask your guides, angels, gods, goddesses, or whoever to help you shift to 5D energy.

3. If that seems too hard, just ride the wave of crappiness and acknowledge, "This is how it is for now. It sucks, but I can work on my energy later if I want to." Then check back in a few hours and see if #1 or #2 seem doable at that point. If they still seem too hard, ride the wave a little longer and check back again.

Don't push yourself to "work hard" to get 5D energy. Don't get down on yourself for not having it already. Just let yourself have a little space to have a problem. It really is okay.

SECTION 4: MANIFESTING SOMETHING SPECIFIC

KNOW THE ENERGY
YOU WANT

Most Law of Attraction books spend a great deal of time on techniques to manifest specific things. They detail many methods, offering lots of rules and tips. They spend most of their time giving instructions to the mind, emotions, and body. That is very typical for 4D manifesting.

In this book, I am concerned with 5D manifesting, not 4D. On the level of 5D, we are dealing with energy and intention, not mental tricks or emotion-revving. Manifesting from 5D is not really a process. It's just an energetic intention. There actually isn't much to say about manifesting from 5D beyond this principle: attune the energy of what you desire.

The "hard part"--if any of this is hard--is learning to sense energy well enough that you can tell what energy you have and what energy you want. That's what the previous sections were all about, in detail. Once you know how to sense your energy, manifesting becomes rather simple. You just intend the energy of what you want, again and again, until it manifests.

On the Earth plane, there are two ways in which you might get what you desire. The first way is through sheer luck. The Earth is a place of mixed vibrations, and you are always running into new energies. You might just randomly run into the thing you want. That was part of the point of Earth--to explore new energies you might not otherwise think of.

Since that way is rather hit-or-miss, conscious, 5D manifestors use another way. Because energy is what creates, we attune the energy of what we desire. This is how the old Law of Attraction tools of visualization, vision boards, affirmations, and so on really work (when they work). You paste a picture of a red sports car on a vision board and, without realizing it, you attune to the *energy* of having that car. You as an energy being sense, attune, and replay that energy through your system, often without any conscious awareness of it.

Sometimes, though, you're in your head as you're making your vision board, or you're pushing yourself to feel syrupy-sweet excited, and then you don't necessarily attune to the energy of the car as you paste it on. Then your board clings to the wall in helpless futility as you drive your old gas-guzzling clunker day in and day out. No fun! Just going through the motions of pasting pictures on a board or excitedly visualizing a vacation without shifting your energy won't do anything. Conscious manifesting requires a shift in energy.

When you consistently attune to the energy of what you want (through whatever method), you eventually receive it.

Do We Even Need Specific Desires?

You don't have to have specific desires. You could just go with the flow and enjoy whatever life brings you.

So long as you're in 5D energy, whatever life brings you will be pretty great most of the time. Since you're still on Planet Earth, you'll still run into the occasional low vibration. You're still mingling at a party of many, many vibrations, and every once in a while you will run into a stinky guest or a spoiled hors d'oevre. But overall, with 5D energy, the things you manifest will be great. It's definitely an option to make your only manifestation goal "joy" or "peace" or the like.

To intentionally manifest something specific, it takes skill in homing in on specific energies. If you don't care about that particular skill--maybe you've already mastered it, or maybe you are just more interested in other things--then your desires tend to be vague and formless. "I just want a happy life." "I just want whatever the Divine wants to give me."

That's a wonderful way to live, but it's not for everyone. Some of us are dreamers. We envision particular dreams and want to create them in real life. It's the difference between declaring, "I want to paint a picture--any old picture," and "I want to paint a dalmatian puppy riding in a wheelbarrow."

If your desire is specific--you don't just want joy or love, you want a trip to Scotland, designer sunglasses, and a private jet--there's usually a reason for it. Getting that *specific* energy is important. It's a part of the cosmos you want to explore.

Know the Energy You Want

To attune a particular energy, it helps to have clarity about why you want it. You can consider the different aspects of the manifestation and figure out which parts really matter to you. Do you want the jet because you love the sensation of flying? Is it more about status and feeling posh? You can sift through the different energies involved and narrow in on the ones that really matter.

Of course, you won't always know why you want something, and that's okay. You don't have to know everything about why you desire what you desire. Sometimes you just want to experience a new energy you've heard about, and that's all there is to it.

But if you can get a little more clarity, you usually home in on the energy more. If your desire is vague, the energy is not called in so well. So many things can match a vague energy! It's like saying, "I want to paint a picture" and ending up with a blob. It's something, and it might even be pretty, but there's not a lot of skill. You don't have to know the "why," but you do need to know the "what": the nature of the energy itself.

What If You Don't Know the Energy You Want Very Well?

If your desired manifestation is something you've had before, like a good cup of coffee or a smooch from a sweetheart, you can probably already attune to that energy. You may not have paid much attention to the energy underneath the last time you had some coffee, but you can probably still remember the experience and sense for the energy beyond all the taste sensations and scents. Manifesting something you've had before is easier, because you already are familiar (at least a little bit) with that energy.

If your desired manifestation is something you've never had before, but it's quite similar to something you *have* had, then you can probably still attune to the new energy. You'll remember the energy of what you did have, and sort of hunt around energetically for what you think the difference might be.

For example, if you want a trip to China and you've never been there, but you have traveled to Japan, you'll intuitively use your energetic experience of your other trip as a jumping-off point. China and Japan will feel different to you energetically, but tuning in to your past trip to Japan will at least get you into the ballpark. Then you can make some tweaks as you explore the energy.

But what if what you want is *very* different from anything you've ever had before? What if you have no idea what the energy of it would even be like? How are you supposed to tune in to an energy you've never experienced? If you've never been out of your little hometown, how do you manifest an exotic trip to Antarctica? It sounds hopeless.

This "hopeless" project of encountering energies we've had zero experience with is actually a large part of the point of Planet Earth. We created a space where we can randomly run into and experience many, many wildly different energies. It's a realm of exploration.

And as we bump around among these energies, we naturally hear about experiences others have had with some energies here on Earth. We might hear someone say, "Hey, whale-watching in Antarctica is really neat! You see beautiful glaciers and whales and feel a pristine side of Earth." That may give you the briefest glimpse of an energy that seems appealing.

"Oh, Antarctica? That sounds great! But I've never even

been out of my hometown...and I've only seen whales in videos...and it's not that cold where I live...How am I ever going to attune to the energy of this trip?" You've caught a glimpse of an energy you think you'll like, but you don't know it well enough to attune it.

We run into conversations, advertising, stories, and other ideas about experiences we've never had but would like to have. And until we can attune to the energy of those experiences more directly, we have to rely on those sources to help us get in the energetic ballpark.

In other words, if you've never had the experience you're looking for, you need to interact with anything that gets you close to that energy. You won't know the exact energy at first--if you did, you'd just attune to it directly. Instead, you have to fumble around, trying different things, sensing the energy underneath, until you finally narrow down the energetic signature of what you want.

You have to know which energies are involved in what you want to manifest. For big, dramatic manifestations, some of those energies will be *new*. That means you will probably need help finding those energies.

That may mean doing research, finding objects that help coach you into the energy, getting to know people who have had that experience or one similar to it, or in some other way just getting access to the experience of the new energies. You probably can't discover all the new energies just from inside your head! You'll need collaboration with the Earth plane. It offers a multitude of different energies, and you'll have to sift through them until you find what you're looking for. And because this big, transformational manifestation is so *new* to you energetically, you won't necessarily know what the energy exactly is before you find it!

If it's a trip to Antarctica you want, that may mean watching more videos, talking to people who have made exotic trips to other places, visiting whale-watching websites, and so on--*while sensing the energy as you do so.*

If all you do is skim photos, it's hit or miss whether you connect with the energy of the trip you want. It's better to notice your energy as you're doing this. "Hmm, I sense expansion and spaciousness when I look at this whale-watching website. But when I look at this other one, I feel kind of constricted. What's the difference here?" "The Arctic is really cold and has whale-watching. Why do I not feel drawn there? Hmm, there's something jangly in my energy when I look at pictures of the Arctic, and something smoother when I look at Antarctica. That's interesting."

Over time, as you practice, you'll get more and more focus on the exact energy you're looking for. It won't always be something you can put into words, but you'll know it intuitively.

Earth is a party of many mixed vibrations. This is an advantage in turning us on to new desires for new experiences, and it's an advantage in helping us manifest those new experiences, because even if we can't attune the energy directly ourselves yet, we can bump around and investigate the various vibrations that feel close. You probably can't instantly attune to Antarctica-ness, but you can read blogs about it or watch movies about it until you learn the energy.

Get to know the exact energy of what you want.

ATTUNE IT

Once you have a general idea of the energy you want, you start attuning to it more often. You can do this in a variety of ways.

Attune to the Energy through Conscious Practice

One way is to use a Law of Attraction technique that resonates with you, being sure to pay attention to your energy rather than just going through the motions.

If it's a big desire, make sure you get to know the new energies involved. If you try to attune to the energy of a big transformation, but you only attune to the energies you're already familiar with, you'll get more of the nice things you're already familiar with but not the big new special thing you wanted.

For example, if you want to get married but you've never even been on a date, there's a lot of energies you're not familiar with that you will need to get in touch with. Just visualizing proposals and attuning to the "romantic" energies you already know may get you some surprise flowers from your mom or a few nice compliments from people you're attracted to. It's not likely to create the big transformation you're hoping for, because you haven't yet discovered what energies you're even seeking in it. There might be a new energy of tingling risk, the feeling of exposing your true self to be known and loved for who you are. Or a new energy of expansive surrender, the kind where you can walk right into a crowded place and declare your love without shame or embarrassment.

Whatever the new energies are, identifying them as best

you can will help you attune to the full experience you desire. Otherwise, you'll just replay the nice energies you already know--which will get you some more pleasant experiences, but nothing major.

Once you know the energy of your desire, do something to embody that energy. You can write a "future journal" describing your trip in the past tense, do a visualization, make a vision board, and so on. Remember that these only work insofar as they actually get you to attune to the desired energy. And remember that to stay in 5D energy, you can't bully yourself into a practice. It needs to feel good energetically while you are doing it. It doesn't have to feel fun in an emotional sense every day, but it does need to feel good deep down--"free" or "solid" or "electric" or whatever way you identify high energy.

It almost doesn't matter what kind of physical, emotional, or mental activity it is--the point is, you are doing the activity with the intention of embodying this very specific energy in your system. You can clap your hands once with this intention, and it's still working the energy. Just play with different methods until you find one that helps you ground the new energy into yourself.

There will be some things you enjoy more than others, or some things that work better for you than others. Embodying energy is something you do all the time without thinking about it. You're creating things all the time. Now you're just making the process more conscious and intentional.

When you're this intentional, the resistant energies that hold you back from your goal get the message and let go. It just becomes very clear, energetically, that you're ready for the journey towards getting what you want to end. You're ready for the finish line.

It's like you're gently demonstrating to all the resistance in your system, "This. This new energy state. This is what we're doing now." And then the resistant energy lets go and coordinates with you. "Oh, this. Sure, I can do this. Didn't know you were ready for that yet."

So that's one way to attune to the energy you desire: practice some technique regularly that helps you sense that energy.

Attune the Energy by Smoothing Out Your Energy While Intending the Topic

If you're not sure of the exact energy of what you want, you can also use the method already described as "The Basic Exercise" in the chapter "Exercises for Practicing Sensing Energy."

In other words, you do the following:

1. Let your body and emotions settle enough that they won't distract you.

2. Sense your current energy.

3. If it's pretty good energy, or at least neutral, then bring to mind the topic of your desired manifestation. (If your energy feels lousy, let it "smooth out" first or come back later.)

4. As you consider your desire, check your energy again. Most of the time, you don't have your desire because some of your energy around that topic is 3D or 4D. Can you sense any energy around you that feels clogged, stinging, sluggish, or [your word of choice for negative energy]?

5. Gently intend that the energy smooth out. (For example, if it feels clogged, intend for the clogs to shift and dissolve. If it feels sluggish, intend for it to start flowing faster.) Make sure you do this gently. If it starts to feel like you're bullying yourself, drop the exercise and come back to it later.

If you wish, you can rev up the process by asking your angels, guides, ancestors, or whoever to help you dissolve the clogs, speed up the sluggish energy, and so on. By releasing the 3D or 4D energy patterns, you make room for 5D energy to flow in fairly naturally.

Attune to the Energy by Finding It Already Existing in Your Life

Another way to attune to the energy consistently is to try

to *find* that energy in your everyday life. It already exists there in bits and pieces. This takes a lot of energetic finesse, but has massive payoffs.

In the Antarctica example, this would mean that you go about your day looking for the Antarctica-trip-energy wherever it may occur. Once you know the exact energetic *feel* of the Antarctica trip, you can recognize it hiding in all kinds of seemingly unrelated things.

Maybe as you're copying documents, you feel the air conditioner kick on and a stream of cold air brush your neck, and deep within, you sense a little of that exotic, chilly wonderland-feeling. Maybe as you're riding the subway and the light dims as you enter a tunnel, you're suddenly reminded of the six months of darkness Antarctica has.

Some things throughout your day may feel rather obviously connected to your dream--seeing an ad for a whale-watching tour on YouTube, or seeing a bumper sticker of a whale, or noticing that your water bottle says "glacier" on it. But it's not the mental matching that we're looking for, remember. It's the energetic feel. If the bumper sticker has the same energy as the Antarctica trip you desire, *that's* what to focus on. Some whale bumper stickers may have the right feel. Others may not. You have to keep checking the energy.

You'll know you know the energy through-and-through when you can sense it in something not obviously connected to your desire. Whale bumper stickers are fine, but what if you sense the same exotic-fun-thrilling-chilly-expansive-electric feeling in the wind chimes your neighbor has outside? There's no obvious mental connection between your trip and the sound of the chimes, but if you notice the same energy running through both, that's a big win!

You might notice the same energy when traffic suddenly eases up and your vehicle zooms forward, or when you hear a child squeal with laughter. You might notice a helpful email from a coworker has a bit of that energy, while a sale ad email has an energy that was exciting but not really Antarctica-trip-like. You'll have to sift through your experiences from an energetic perspective to notice which good energies match your Antarctic dream and which are high-vibrational but not really a match.

This Antarctica-trip-energy will not occur in every happy or high-vibrational moment, or even most of them--but the energy is already lurking in your life somewhere. There will be tiny pockets of experience throughout your day that have this energy. Whatever it means to you, find it in tiny ways throughout your day.

As you get better and better at sensing energy in general, and as you get better and better at knowing this Antarctica-trip-energy, you'll discover bits and pieces of it throughout your ordinary life. And then you feel closer to it, and attune to it more keenly and more often, and then your manifestation speeds along into your lap.

But you have to pay subtle attention to events, places, people, and so on to find the energy you want. It's not obvious how Antarctic-whale-watching-energy is in the Pentagon. It's not clear how it's in the Friday night news. Finding the energy takes some patience and willingness to see it in odd places. You will gradually change the places you go and the things you do as you notice where you find the energy. Maybe you stop hanging around the Pentagon so much because you don't feel much Antarctica-wonderland energy there. Maybe you do more crocheting or rock climbing because it's easier to find that energy there. Who knows? It will depend on your own experiences.

Paying close enough attention to the energy of what you want to sense it when it shows up can be tough! I don't want to downplay that. How do you sense the energy of an exotic trip, besides looking at travel brochures or watching videos of people doing that? And yet the energy is all over the place, in little pockets here and there, because there's a deeper nuance to it. You can notice where it pops up in your day. "Oh! That billboard with a glitzy picture actually feels a little like the trip I want!" "Oh!

That kiss from my sweetheart felt a little bit like it, too."

After you are good at sensing the energy, it's much easier to intend it. And the more consistently you intend it, the faster it comes. Can you see how difficult it is if you don't know exactly what the energy feels like? How do you make filing papers feel like a whale-watching vacation? It seems hopeless if you haven't been noticing the tiny bits of that energy in billboards and kisses.

Do We Even Need the Physical Manifestation?

You might wonder, "If we can get this energy in so many places, then why bother with the manifestation at all?"

Indeed, many Law of Attraction writers insist that you should enjoy your internal experience so much that you don't even care if your dream ever happens in the "real world." If visualizing smooching your sweetheart satisfies you entirely, then by all means, enjoy that. But the Earth experience was created for (among other things) a physical experience of energy. So if some part of you feels annoyed or judged when you're not satisfied with the daydreams and visualizations, there's a good reason for that. The physical aspect is part of what Earth is all about.

The LOA writers who insist we should be satisfied with our daydreams do have a point--energy is what causes your manifestation, and that's something internal. And if you're attuning the energy of what you want well, it will usually feel really good emotionally. (Usually. Refer back to "How Emotions and Energy Sensations are Different" for clarification on that.)

Saying you should be satisfied with the internal experience of your dream rather than still wanting its outward manifestation is like saying artists should be satisfied with thinking of a painting rather than putting paint on canvas. On Earth, we're here to create in the physical. If we were truly satisfied by only imagining things, we would not have bothered to have bodies in the first place.

Some dreams may be satisfied by a happy daydream, but if

you want more, attune the energy of that dream to manifest it physically.

WHAT IF YOU'RE STILL HAVING TROUBLE SENSING ENERGY?

What if you've tried and tried to sense energy, but still are having trouble doing it?

If you've settled down your emotions and body sensations, and let your thoughts be like white noise in the background, and despite doing all this, you don't sense anything underneath, that is very common. That is the default state for human beings in a 3D world. Energy is natural to you as a soul, but as a human on Planet Earth, it is hidden at first so that you can have the experience of long, drawn-out journeys to your manifestations. If sensing energy were in-your-face and obvious, we'd figure out how to manifest what we want super quickly and the game of Earth would be up.

We're getting closer to the end of that game, so eventually it *will* be very easy for everyone. In time, Earth will be a piece of cake rather than a challenging game. But for now, there are still illusions and tricky bits to manage.

The fact that you intellectually know that energy is at the bottom of your creations is a great first step. You will begin to sense energy in the future. All of us who continue on Planet Earth will eventually reach this point. But in the meantime, while you're still feeling a bit befuddled, it helps to keep three things in mind:

1. You can still make progress with your manifestations

using the old-fashioned Law of Attraction teachings.

It won't be as smooth and direct as working with energy, but you can still get some results with visualization, feeling the emotions you'd have with your manifestation now, and so on. As you practice these old techniques, you'll notice that sometimes they work and sometimes they don't. With each round of trial and error, you'll be learning about the energetic state underneath.

For the most part, this learning will be subconscious. Since you can't sense the energy consciously, you might not know what energy is producing which results consciously. But your subconscious will still be learning, and it will prompt you through intuition to do more of what is working. "Do that technique again--that seemed to work a little...No, not quite like that. It felt different the last time we did it. Try it this way...Yes, that's better."

Although all of us are sensing energy all the time, it's not conscious for most of us. Learning how to sense it consciously can take time.

Some energy workers and mediums have beautiful stories of how they could sense energy and otherworldly beings even as children. I don't have a story like that. Although I was always good at sensing emotion, I didn't even know that sensing energy was a thing until I was in college.

I didn't have a guru to guide me, and the books at the time simply said the LOA was all about emotion and thought. I had to learn about energy the slow, trial-and-error way, just noticing how sometimes the happy feelings and visualizations felt "right" and got results, and sometimes the same happy feelings and visualizations felt off and didn't work. Then I had to figure out what the difference was. That led me to sensing energy underneath--first as vague glimpses, and then gradually as a consistent and noticeable thing.

It's a longer, slower road using trial and error and subconscious learning, but you will still be making progress in learning about energy. Eventually you will get better and better intuitive hits, and then eventually you will begin to get the sense of the energy itself as your intuition cues you.

2. All over the world, individuals are learning more about energy. For every person who learns to sense it a tiny bit better, it makes it easier for the next person to learn that. And the next, and the next.

Whether you call it the collective unconscious, morphogenic fields, or the Hundredth Monkey effect, one person learning something helpful makes it easier for others to learn the same thing *even if they never say a word about it.*

Planet Earth herself is learning and growing, too. She is creating an energetic atmosphere for us. As she evolves, her energy supports us in evolving more and more. Her high-vibrational energies are shifting even higher, making really awesome energy and information available to us, more and more at every moment. So Planet Earth's own energies are making it easier and easier for us to grow in these ways.

As other self-aware beings learn to sense energy, it becomes easier for you to do so. As the Earth evolves, it becomes easier for you to evolve. Even if you don't practice at all, sensing energy will become easier and easier with time. What Earth herself is doing and what other people are doing benefits you.

3. You can also try out a different LOA perspective. Since your signature vibration is unique, no other person's view on energy will exactly match your own. But the way one person describes it may get a little closer than the way a different person describes it.

The words used, the metaphors--even the examples may resonate more with you coming from one source rather than another. If my words and descriptions don't help you get very close, someone else's perspective might.

There are many excellent LOA theories and exercises out there. It may just be that you haven't found one that resonates closely enough to help you sense energy. I've found many LOA books useful, even if I don't totally agree with everything they say. Richard Dotts' *Instantly Directed Manifestations*, Melody

Fletcher's *Deliberate Receiving*, and Erin Werley's *Lightworkers 101* are just some of the books I've found helpful. And there are many more blogs, vlogs, websites, and books to explore. Take what works for you and leave the rest.

In the end, your understanding of energy will be unique to you. But as you're getting started, you may have to shuffle around and try a few different theories or explanations until you find something that resonates with you well enough to put time into. Later, even that awesome theory will have a few wrinkles for you, and you'll wind up adjusting their theories and techniques to suit yourself.

If you're eager to manifest more consciously faster and you're having trouble with this material, try a different author's perspective. You may discover you come back to this material later, when you are better able to sense energy--or you may find you go off in a whole new direction. Either way, it can be helpful to explore.

IN CLOSING

So now we've made the bare-bones journey of how to create manifestations with energy. Most of our time was spent on understanding what energy is like and how to sense it, because that tends to be the tricky part for human beings.

To recap, on Planet Earth, we are in a place of mixed vibrations. There is a heck of a lot of 3D energy, some 4D energy, some 5D energy, and many free-willed players on the field.

All the 3D energy is useful in slowing down our journey from *wanting something* to *getting it*. But now most of us are finished playing the long, drawn-out stories of struggle we began with. Now we want to manifest our dreams more quickly and easily.

That means we need to shift the parts of our lives that are stuck in 3D to a higher vibration. Shifting to 4D is nice, but it's covered by many, many other books and modalities. That's why I've focused on the shift to 5D, which is newer to most of us and not as well covered.

To sense energy, you'll have to develop your own vocabulary of what things feel like to you. Energy is something different and deeper than thoughts, emotions, and body sensations. That means it helps to quiet down your body, mind, and emotions when you're practicing sensing energy. You can practice by getting quiet and checking in. You can also practice by noticing when you sense a mismatch. Maybe your body feels great, but you sense something's off underneath. Or maybe your emotions feel crummy, but you sense something powerful and expansive underneath them.

Once you're able to sense energy, it becomes easier to

move towards 5D. The main methods we covered for shifting to 5D energy were: asking high-vibrational beings for help shifting, spreading 5D vibes from an area of your life that's going swimmingly to a problem area, and engaging in an energetic attitude that faces our crummy 3D pattern without trying to mess with it (curiosity, trust, surrender, humor, and so on). We also noted that judgyness and bullying yourself are 3D energies that are important to let go of.

Stopping there--just accessing more 5D energy--is fine. If you'd like to hone in on a particular manifestation more, however, you can do so by: 1. Knowing the specific energy of the thing you want, and 2. Attuning that energy.

Knowing the exact energy you want sometimes requires exploration. You may not be able to figure it all out in your head. You may need to interact with others, watch videos, check websites, or otherwise explore the world more to get more of an idea what energy is involved in what you want.

Once you know the energy, you can begin attuning it directly. You can do this through performing some activity that helps you get in touch with that energy, smoothing out your energy as you sense the hiccups or clogs in it around that topic, or by looking for that energy wherever it pops up in your day-to-day life.

Originally, *A Maverick's Guide to the Law of Attraction* was one enormous book. Once I realized I had over 100,000 words of content, I realized it really needed to be split into at least two books.

I scraped the bare-bones idea down as best I could and presented it here in Book 1. Book 2 will contain ideas I think are helpful but not as necessary: your signature vibration as a soul, the story of the Earth experiment, how free will works, suggestions for empaths, and troubleshooting tough manifestation cases. If you've enjoyed this book and would like more, please consider moving on to Book 2. But the basic things you need to know are here in Book 1.

And as always, **take what works for you and leave the**

rest. Your path of manifestation will always have uniqueness to it, and there will always be moments where honoring yourself requires ditching what the "experts" say.

Happy manifesting!

IF YOU ENJOYED THIS BOOK...

...please rate and review it at Amazon, Goodreads, or your social media of choice.

This helps others find the book, and it helps me to know if readers would enjoy more of this kind of content.

You can also look for *A Maverick's Guide to the Law of Attraction, Book 2: Why We're Here, How We Got Here, and What to Do about It* at Amazon.

Thank you!

ABOUT THE AUTHOR

Lisa Rasche

Lisa Rasche is a long-time fan of metaphysical and other "woo woo" books. Not only that, but she has a doctorate in philosophy, so she's no stranger to analysis. She seeks to combine intuition and logical rigor in the paradoxical pursuit of exploring deep reality.

Her first book was a playful work of fiction, The Birthday Parties of Dragons. As Elizabeth Rasche, she has written a number of romantic fiction books, including Flirtation and Folly, A Learned Romance, The Pink Daffodil, and Kitty Bennet's Midsummer.

Lisa lives in Arkansas with her husband and cat.

BOOKS IN THIS SERIES

A Maverick's Guide To The Law Of Attraction, Book 2: Deep Dives

If you're ready to swim the depths of the Law of Attraction...A Maverick's Guide to the Law of Attraction, Book 2: Deep Dives is for you.

While Book 1 focused on the basics of manifesting with energy, Book 2 dives deeper into particular topics, background, and theory.

The first deep dive goes into your signature vibration—your soul's specific frequency—and how to use it to manifest. At your core, you are energy. You exist as a specific "flavor" of energy, and that can help you create what you want in life.

The second dive explores why we came to Earth in the first place, and the surprising difficulties that emerged when powerful souls restricted parts of themselves as egos. It turns out that egos are people, too!

The third deep dive is free will. Given that we are sovereign souls with free will, how do we actually affect each other? Do we create everything in our lives, or do others have a say in our creations? Do we have to experience everything we want to know ourselves, directly?

The final deep dive troubleshoots tough manifestations. Why are some manifestations particularly tricky? What energies might be missing from your dream? And what about the really bad stuff in life that appears out of nowhere?

These four topics are really about why we are here, how we got here, and what to do about it. There's more to manifestation and Planet Earth than parking spaces and gold rings. There's a larger, deeper story...and there's so much more to explore as mavericks.

BOOKS BY THIS AUTHOR

Flirtation And Folly

Marianne Mowbrey is a responsible country rector's daughter who longs for the novelty and excitement she reads about in novels. When her crusty Aunt Harriet agrees to give her a Season in London, Marianne vows to dazzle the world, win a husband, and never go home again.

But the Londoners who determine social success are inclined to pass over plain Marianne in favor of her beautiful, reckless younger sister. In a world of ambition, fashion, flattery, and deceit, how can Marianne stay true to her real self—when she is not even sure what that real self is?

A Learned Romance

MARY BENNET HAD NEVER WISHED for anything more than to be known as the meek and pious Bennet sister, the one who sweetly brought peace to her family.

BEING THE LAST UNMARRIED BENNET SISTER, the pressure to partake of a London Season with the nouveau riche Wickhams was considerable, no matter how little she desired it; her younger sister Lydia would not hear a refusal. Mary hoped she could pass her days as quietly as a mouse and maybe encourage her still-wild sister to become a more demure wife and stop quarrelling so much with her husband.

BUT WHEN LYDIA'S FLIRTATION with a scientist begins stirring gossip, Mary discovers it is not enough to stay meek and quiet. She must protect Lydia's reputation by drawing the man's attentions her way, and convincing the world it is Mary, not Lydia, who attracts Mr Cole. If she fails, Lydia's disgrace will taint every family member connected with her—Bennet, Bingley, and Darcy alike—and Mary will have no hope for her own future. But alluring a gentleman is hardly the sort of practice Mary has a knack for. Though it goes against every fibre of her being, Mary must turn aside from the peace she craves and uncover the belle within—all while finding her heart awakening in the illusion of romance she has created.

A LEARNED ROMANCE is a sequel to Jane Austen's beloved Pride and Prejudice.

The Pink Daffodil

CHRISTMAS MAY MEAN FESTIVITY and fun for some, but for Mary Bennet it is an opportunity to collect donations for her Meryton Widows and Orphans Society. Mary is eager to display her piety and charity to everyone around her in the small town of Meryton, but finds herself distracted by the arrival of Mr Arthur at Netherfield Park. A friend of Mr Bingley, he is an awkward gentleman in shabby attire who cheerfully disregards etiquette to an alarming degree—and yet Mary finds him endearing nevertheless.

WITH THE YULETIDE FROLICS come the opportunity for both diversion and discovery—discovery that Mr Arthur is not what or who he seems to be, and the understanding for Mary that sometimes pious is not the only thing she wants to be.

THE PINK DAFFODIL is a sequel to Jane Austen's Pride and Prejudice and will be enjoyed by fans of Miss Mary Bennet.

Kitty Bennet's Midsummer

Having been partners in folly with her sister Lydia all her life, Kitty Bennet finds herself at a loss when Lydia elopes and Kitty is left to endure the new strictures of their father. Longbourn seems unbearably quiet with only her pious sister Mary for company. Kitty longs for any foolish adventure, but her father's sternness insists on another dull summer at home.

Kitty solaces herself with long rambles in the woods and reveries of fairies. When a simple gift seems to transform the forest into a place of magic, Kitty begins to question her sanity. The arrival of a cloaked foreigner, Bren, makes Kitty's summer even stranger. Bren's tales of the Fae realm seem a little too detailed to be mere stories—and yet, how can Kitty believe that such things exist?

When Kitty embraces the magic enough to make a reckless wish, the consequences prove her foolishness and endanger her family. Now she must hasten to reckon with the fateful magic. Kitty must find her own sort of wisdom to aid Bren, help her family, and stand tall in her own life.

Can one summer transform a foolish, petulant girl into a young woman of heart? All it takes is a little magic.

The Birthday Parties Of Dragons

In the strict society of dragons, becoming an adult means everything. For only adult dragons are fearsome enough to dazzle human minds into forgetfulness, thereby keeping dragons safely within the realms of myth and mystery.

But for one young dragon named Ittle, time is running out. Dragons must become large and monstrous enough by their one hundredth birthdays to be considered adults or face exile and disgrace. And despite his utmost efforts, Ittle simply cannot grow.

Facing a life of embarrassment with the possibility of becoming an exiled hatchling, Ittle attends a grueling finishing school as a last-ditch effort. Unfortunately, even the regimen of the school fails to make him grow.

As desperation sets in, Ittle decides the only way to prove his strength is by undertaking a daring duel with another dragon— a sure disaster. But just as all hope seems lost, Ittle is faced with the chance to become an unlikely hero to save another dragon's life and prove all those who doubt him wrong.

THE BIRTHDAY PARTIES OF DRAGONS is a tale of a misfit dragon in the pursuit of self-acceptance and confidence whose mission will prove that fearsomeness comes in all sizes.

A Maverick's Guide To The Law Of Attraction, Book 2: Deep Dives

If you're ready to swim the depths of the Law of Attraction...A Maverick's Guide to the Law of Attraction, Book 2: Deep Dives is for you.

While Book 1 focused on the basics of manifesting with energy, Book 2 dives deeper into particular topics, background, and theory.

The first deep dive goes into your signature vibration—your soul's specific frequency—and how to use it to manifest. At your core, you are energy. You exist as a specific "flavor" of energy, and that can help you create what you want in life.

The second dive explores why we came to Earth in the first place, and the surprising difficulties that emerged when powerful souls restricted parts of themselves as egos. It turns out that egos are people, too!

The third deep dive is free will. Given that we are sovereign souls with free will, how do we actually affect each other? Do we create everything in our lives, or do others have a say in our creations? Do we have to experience everything we want to know ourselves, directly?

The final deep dive troubleshoots tough manifestations. Why are some manifestations particularly tricky? What energies might be missing from your dream? And what about the really bad stuff in life that appears out of nowhere?

These four topics are really about why we are here, how we got here, and what to do about it. There's more to manifestation and Planet Earth than parking spaces and gold rings. There's a larger, deeper story…and there's so much more to explore as mavericks.